"THE COMEDIAN"

(Look who's laughing now)

Knowledge Is Learned

K.I.L.

Angela M. Smith

The opinions expressed in this manuscript are solely the opinions of the authors Angela M. Smith and do not represent the opinions or thoughts of the publisher. The author has warranted full ownership and/or legal right to publish all of the material and content in this book. Only the author can give consent for any use of content in this book.

ACKNOWLEDGMENTS

First of all, I give thanks to God, in your son Jesus name you give me the vision to continue the journey for you are my strength and my salvation, for without you there would be no me. Father, bless those who have and those who have not, because you are the true provider.

To Andrew, (A Lie Will Not Stand), the fight for your name continues, God favors you and the Victory is coming. No weapon formed shall prosper. It just won't work. The race for the Grammy continues I love you.

Andre, it is truly time for you to shine, don't let anyone hold you back. Your dreams are yours go and get it. The race for the Grammy continues for you too. You have too much talent to sit idle. Make a Move Kid, the world is yours. I love you

Kai Renee- Mom-mom loves you. Also Know that your daddy loves you so much, Integrity is everything. Watch all trust none, baby girl. I love you☺

My brothers:
Steven- being the oldest you have shown me a lot thx, Mark the middle isn't so bad, and Joe the youngest was a great spot, thank you for always being here for me. My nieces and nephews, "Kitty" (Rest in heaven), Tiffany, Stevie, Shawn, Gary, Jessica, Sierra, Mark Jr. & Josiah. I love you and we will continue to move forward and support each other thru life,

To my grandmother (Freddie Lee) "Now you are with my mom, may God watch over both of you now, my aunts, Patricia, and Wendy, (Irene), (Edna), and uncles Samuel, Stan & Calvin, dad, cousins and friends, thank you for your continued support on my journey. I love you.

CSK – Luv U Thanks for being the vessel God used to help me get through Covid I appreciate you.

Rumble B- It's been a journey well worth the wait Tracy- BFF for life, Michelle D. Linda D. our stories are priceless.

Lee (Bill Collectors) Adam (EMT Radio) Larry Larr, EST, Sheila Clinton, Pete Lyde, Terry, Danita, Angela T. Eric H. Herb G. it's too many of you to name, thank you so much for your continued support.

DEDICATIONS

Priscilla Rose Conover-Smith-Shepherd- It has been a long 10 years with you watching over me, and I want you to know that my journey continues. I love you and I know you will continue to watch over us and guide us through this life. R.I.P (Paradise)

Priscilla Rose is a beautiful name,
And the woman that wore it was a beautiful frame,
Portrait ready every moment of her life,
A wonderful daughter, sister, mother, and wife

Dreams she wanted never really came true,
She didn't believe in herself enough
To let them shine through.

Now she watches me daily
And she reminds me of mine
Letting me know that it's my time to shine.

Mother I hear you and I know life is too short
To not make my dreams come true
With your enduring support
I hear your whispers and I know you are there
Still supporting my goals and still being here

You can do it Angie
That is what you would say
You are going to make it
Your dreams are your way

Intro

Let me introduce you to Marcus Hall. Tall dark and handsome, nice smile, nice build, smooth talk, and one of the best fucks you will ever experience in life. The things he does in the bedroom, is a true connection.

As I take you on this journey you will understand how Maria stayed in lust for so many years. Who wants a no-good cheating mutha fucka, (raise your hand ladies, some of you are living it every single day) and the worse part is you don't even know it!

I take that back. Some of you do know it and allow it and accept it. We all have fallen for a Marcus Hall. Just pray we have outgrown, the risky sex and the oral cum that makes you scream at the top of your fucking lungs. (Flash back) oh my goodness. Is it me or is it hot in here?

This man has a dick that is so right. It's the kind of dick that talks to your pussy at the door. As the key turns your body just knows. Your clit starts to thrust, and your walls start to clinch because daddy's home. Yeah daddy, bring that big dick over here. Yes, Maria was hooked. And so was Sharon, Monique and Kaye, Lisa, and Rose, etc. let me take you into the journey of the Comedian.

Two Faced'

Everybody tries to get through life without you
Two Faced
Everybody knows one they get discouraged when
they meet one
Two Faced
And so the story begins:

Ten years ago, and ever so blind
I met two faced
And I never thought I'd find
Someone so dear
Someone so true
I should have known he wasn't for real
Because I met him in a court room

He never took me on a date he just came over to
basically conversate
And see what he could get into
My head, my pants, my sexual woo

He lived at home
In a thirty-foot square room
And he's never moved out, so I assume
Because up until this very day
Two faced lives in the same place

The same mirrors are on the wall
The same dresser is standing tall
The very same rug is on the floor
To accommodate some fresh young whore

I finally got into him
When I got back from out of town
If I had known any better
I would have left him
Where he was found

I fell in love, I fell in lust
And slowly I began to trust
His every word, his every touch
Just loving him so very much

Slowly he began to be
My heart my world my everything
Two faced had me dangling on
Another heartbroken love song

He began to pay the rent
So I thought he was heaven sent
But then he began to tell me lies
Blinded by love
I did not recognize

The hurt and pain
That would surely come
When I knew where two faced
Was coming from

Girls began to call my home
And two faced left me all alone
To argue on the telephone
Knowing that his shit was wrong

Though he still paid the rent
He was no longer heaven sent
But surely, he was cast from hell
By the way his shit stunk and smelled

He gave me everything
But love and quality time
The things that made me feel just fine
No candlelight, no wine and dine
I surely knew he was not mine

The love that use to feel my heart
Quickly began to fall apart
No car, no ring, no wedding date
For he, and I it was just too late

On my knees I began to pray
And leave my prayers in God's grace
For I could no longer stand to chase
The one side love
Known as Two Faced···

The Table of Contents

The Table of Contents

CHAPTER ONE

"The Beginning"

It was a hot summer day, and Maria was on her way to object to a restraining order that had been placed against her with the Philadelphia Courts. She wore an orange Capri Set, to show her shapely curves, her hair was medium length with slight curls to reflect her oval face and slanted eyes her skin was caramel shade with a slight tone of bronze.

As she entered the court room, all eyes were on her. She walked up to the court clerk, gave her name and then took a seat and waited to be called.

After about ten minutes of waiting, she noticed a young man starring at her hard, she glanced up at him and they made eye contact, he then began to slide several chairs towards her.

Maria really wasn't in the mood for meeting anyone, but at the same time this young man was handsome, and of course she was wondering why he was there, after all this was the stay away order court.

As he came closer, Maria said hello, as he said hello at the same time, He said my name is Marcus Hall, she replied my name is Maria Smalls. They instantly connected and exchanged pager numbers,

Marcus was about 5'9 brown skinned with black hair and dark bedroom eyes, Maria instantly thought wow he is really a good -looking man.

As they began to converse some more the court clerk started to call the next case, "Maria Smalls" "the court clerk called" Maria stood up and replied yes as she walked into the next room where the judge and the man with the order to be placed against her stood.

The young man with the restraining order request name was Joey Scales, a man she had met several months a go, Joey was about 5'8 light skinned and a bit frail, not a real looker. They had begun dating and things didn't go so well because Joey was a cheater and Maria just wasn't having that so new in a relationship.

Joey had obtained a restraining order against Maria based on an argument from a few days prior, he had left some things over Maria's apartment and wanted them back, but because of Maria's brother Joey felt the need to get a restraining order so he wouldn't have to deal with her brother, while obtaining his articles.

They did not live together but he had stayed a night or two before Maria realized what a loser he was.

As Joey told his story about trying to obtain his belongings Maria nodded in agreement to the judge and said yes it isn't safe for him to come where I live, and if he doe's he will get what he is coming for.

The judge granted Joey's order based on Maria's responses, Maria agreed to return the young man's articles and be done with him. After they completed the paperwork, the clerk gave the final order and they where both on their separate ways.

As Maria left the courthouse she noticed Marcus outside, she went up to him and they began walking towards the train and talking, Marcus started saying how he normally drives but because this was downtown on Filbert Street, he didn't want to end up in a lot of traffic, so he just took the el train.

Maria as well took the train into town the Broad Street line. They lived in two different parts of the city, Marcus from West Philly and Maria from the Logan part of the city. They parted at City Hall and went their separate ways.

Maria had reached her stop at Logan on the broad street line as she came up the steps and walked several blocks down to pick up her son, Eric from day care, Eric was about three years old, and was an amazing little kid.

He was always fascinated by just seeing his mother smile, as they walked towards their apartment, Eric just kept asking mom smile again, your smile is so pretty, Maria loved that Eric knew that a smile just meant she was happy. I think he really enjoyed her smile,

Later that evening Marcus paged Maria, she didn't have a phone, so she would run out to the phone booth outside of her apartment and call him back, the phone booth had a return number so Maria was able to give Marcus that number to contact her on.

After several weeks of talking back and forth to Marcus, they finally went on a date to a movie, after the movie, they came back to Maria's place and just chilled.

As they sat there talking Marcus tried to have sex with Maria, but she was not ready at that time. Even though she had been thinking of the date and time that it would happen she just wasn't ready. She kissed Marcus good night and sent him home, he had continuously called her pager trying to come back over but Maria didn't respond.

Maria lived in a small one bedroom, apartment in a part of the city called Logan. It was a cute little spot for her and Eric to flourish into their being. Maria had to move out of her mothers, place upon having Eric, her mom was strict to the rule that two women could not live in the same house. Maria was now a woman on her own with a little one.

Maria worked as an Administrative Assistant to make a living for her and Eric, while also attending beauty school in center city. She wasn't really sure about the beauty school once she hit the clinic floor and found out how much hair equipment was going to cost.

Maria got cold feet and decided to change her profession and went to school for Community Health Instructor instead. She also dipped in the bartending scene for a minute to keep her grounded and more money in her pocket.

Maria was very independent and very serious about her and Eric's future. She was a hard worker and didn't depend on anyone for anything. She was beautiful she could have had any man she wanted if he wanted her.

The one thing she couldn't stand was a cheater. And she made it very clear upon meeting and dating that she was not a cheater and did not want to be cheated on.

Several days later Maria finally decided to call Marcus back, Maria and Eric ended up on a date with Marcus. They went out to dinner at Outback steak house, and then went to Dairy queen for dessert.

While driving home Eric asked to stop at game stop to buy a game, Marcus pulled over and they went in to purchase a game.

Money was never a problem for Marcus, so, more dates came along with endless, roses, candy, and help with Maria's bills.

CHAPTER TWO

"Getting to know you"

About several months into the relationship Marcus finally took Maria over to his place. He lived in a four -bedroom house in West Philly with his mom, stepdad, and his little brother.

As Maria looked around the house, she didn't notice many pictures of family around, she also didn't notice any thongs or female items in Marcus room,

Marcus's mom had cooked and offered them to stay and have some dinner. Upon saying yes Marcus older brother Mod entered the house with his girlfriend Lena. Lena had a beautiful vase in her hand filled with flowers and candy for Marcus's mom.

She gave her the vase and hugged her, and we all sat down and had dinner. About an hour later Mod left to take Lena home and then came back about fifteen minutes later with another woman.

As they sat in the living room the young lady got up and admired the vase that Lena had given to Mod's mom. The young lady's name was Madeline.

As Marcus mom got up Madeline asked who got her such a beautiful vase, she turned to Marcus and said Maria just gave that to me.

Maria looked up and was shocked to be put in the middle of a lie so quickly. Before Maria could respond, Marcus said yes Madeline Maria and I gave that to my mom today.

Madeline replied, I wish my husband would buy me some flowers sometimes, isn't that right babe, while looking at Mod.

Maria looked at Marcus with an attitude at that point because she didn't know Mod was married and she felt stupid standing there while being placed in a lie at the same time.

Her red flag should have gone up then. But Maria didn't want to judge Marcus by his family's rudeness. At this point Maria was ready to go home, she turned to Marcus and said babe I'm tired let's call it a night.

Marcus stared at Maria and replied yes babe, let me grab your things and I will take you and Eric home. Maria and Eric said their goodbyes, and then got into Marcus Infinity and he drove them home.

On the drive home, Maria tried to question Marcus on the Lena Madeline thing with Mod, but Marcus just replied that is my brother and his mess I don't get involved. Maria said Okay but that's going to blow up in his face one day and I don't want any part of it, and neither should you.

Marcus agreed, as they pulled up to Maria's place, Marcus was pitching his bid to spend the night. Maria said she wasn't ready for all that and Marcus just got out and walked her and Eric to the door and left.

As Maria turned the key, she was wondering why Marcus left so quickly without being a little more aggressive to spending the night, after all they had been seeing each other now for about four months and she felt it was time, she just didn't want to rush into anything.

As her and Eric got settled in their pajamas Marcus was on Maria's pager. She refused to go outside and call him. So, she ended up ignoring him and going to sleep.

Her pager was still vibrating when her alarm clock went off. By this time Maria jumped up got her and Eric ready for the day and off they went to do their daily routine of daycare and work.

By the time Maria got home Marcus was waiting at her door. He had roses in one hand and dinner in the other he was a man that recognized a woman's hard day at work. Maria's face lit up with a smile and she was so happy that Marcus thought of her and Eric.

They sat down at the table said grace and started eating. After dinner Maria helped Eric with his homework and got him settled in for bed. She got comfortable too and came and sat on the couch next to Marcus.

They watched a TV show and then Marcus reached over and kissed Maria on the lips. Maria wasn't sure how to react at first and she also didn't want their first time together to be at her place. After all Eric was in the next room and Maria was uncomfortable because of that.

Marcus reached over again and kissed Maria and this time she didn't resist she just thought ok we can kiss. Marcus started to French kiss at this point and Maria was fine with that also.

The next thing she knew she was wet she felt her pussy walls clinching and Marcus was sucking on her breast and his fingers were rubbing her clit and finger fucking her pussy. She still did not resist because it had been a while since she actually had any action.

As Marcus started to work his way down to Maria's pussy with his mouth is when Maria said "wait" I don't want to do it here. Marcus continued with his fingers gliding across her clit and Maria was so wet, but she stuck to what she said. She got up and told Marcus it was time for him to leave.

As they walked to the door Marcus started kissing Maria again, but this time Maria decided to feel on Marcus pants to see what she would eventually be working with.

As Marcus sucked her breast this time Maria grabbed his thickness and started kissing him around his neck. She squeezed it and caressed it as he finger fucked her some more and they both began to wish they were some place else, where they could enjoy the pleasure.

Maria liked what she felt, but again stopped to let Marcus know once more that it was not going down at her place yet. Marcus shook his head kissed Maria's forehead and left for the night.

After Marcus exit, Maria went into the bathroom and finished off the pleasure she wishes she had finished off with Marcus. She cleaned herself up and went to bed thinking of how the penetration of Marcus would really feel when they got to that point. She almost released her juices again thinking about Marcus and the thickness of his dick. She fell asleep, wondering.

As Marcus pulled up to his place, he had the same thoughts, he went into the house and into his room thinking about Maria and feeling his hand with his thick dick and rubbing it with thoughts of her on his mind until he released his pleasure.

He too went to sleep wondering about how his dick would feel penetrating Maria's soft wet pussy, he was thinking about how he placed his fingers into her pussy and finger fucked her, he was licking his lips because he knew how much he wanted to lick and suck her pussy and swallow, her juices from her body.

He was so lusting for her with these thoughts, until his pager vibrated and took him out of his daze. As Marcus looked down at his pager it was an ex-friend of his that he use to get down with. He didn't call her back because he was really thinking about Maria and didn't want to sleep with anyone else until he got to feel Maria's pussy with his thick dick. Marcus rolled over in his waterbed and fell asleep wondering.

Marcus alarm went off at 4:00am because he had to be up and at work by 5. Marcus worked in a Janitorial service and his shift was 5:00am to 1:00pm he was very much dedicated to his job, and he made a very nice salary doing it. And because he lived home with his mother, he saved his money to be able to spend it on the ladies.

He was dedicated to nothing but the game, he was addicted to sex, and he loved different flavors and different taste, when it came down to pleasing the pussy, I don't think a woman he had ever been with could ever complain.

He was very nicety with it. He loved to suck and lick pussy's but never really wanted to French kiss. Marcus was very interested in pleasing his partner.

Later Maria would find out just how many partners existed, but until then the thoughts of Marcus and Maria on each others mind was very, very interesting. Nicety.

CHAPTER THREE

"It's Going Down"

"Ring" ring rang the telephone booth outside of Maria's apartment. She heard it through her window. As she jumped out of bed and threw on some Roc a wear sweats and headed out the door. Maria answered the telephone booth "hello" Marcus said Hey what's up? Maria said how did you know? it would be me, he replied I know your sexy voice,

She laughed and they continued to talk on the phone for about an hour before Marcus said hey let me come and pick you up and go grab something to eat. Maria said sure why not. They hung up the phone and Marcus was on his way. As Maria waited, she started to jump in the shower and wash up and get ready.

She changed her clothes to a pretty blue and white Capri set with some matching, colored sneakers and costume jewelry to set it off. When Marcus knocked on the door and Maria opened it he wasn't disappointed at all. He said wow you look nice, she replied always. As they got into the car Marcus put on R-Kelly bump and grind,

Maria nodded her head to the beat as they pulled off on their way to the diner to get a bite to eat. Eric was with his father, so Maria didn't have to worry about him until Monday, so her mind was relaxed and chilled.

As they arrived at the diner, Maria ordered a glass of orange juice and the #1 special which was cheese grits, eggs over medium, two slices of bacon and two sausages, with wheat toast and butter with jelly.

Marcus ordered steak with two scrabbled eggs with cheese, and a side of home fries. They sat there and enjoyed the meal, and when they where ready to go Marcus paid the waitress and left her a generous tip. That was just his style. Maria smiled and was very happy that Marcus understood and appreciated hard work.

As Maria and Marcus left the diner, Marcus told her he had a surprise for her, he reached behind his seat and pulled out a dozen roses. Maria was very happy.

As they pulled out of the diner lot, he started driving in a different direction than Maria's apartment they ended up at a hotel on City Line Ave. As they pulled into the hotel lot Maria was wondering where this was headed. Sure enough, she was about to find out.

As Marcus pulled a hotel key from his pocket, Maria knew it was a planned get away for the two of them. As they walked through the hotel lobby, hugging, and pecking each other lips, Maria knew it was going down.

As they entered the hotel room, Maria looked around and was amazed at what Marcus had in store there was fresh fruit on trays on the bed, strawberry's melon, pineapple, and apples. On another tray sat chocolate, caramel, and vanilla. On another tray sat shrimp, cocktail sauce, and crab cakes. There were balloons and flower pedals along with candy spread through out the room.

Maria was so happy that Marcus was flattered enough to be this creative. Last but not least was a box with a sexy night shirt and some thongs. Maria quickly went to the shower and washed and changed into the set. Marcus took a shower after her. Maria sat wondering if she should have just taken a shower with him. But then thought no he'll be fine.

As Marcus came out of the shower, he was dripping wet with a towel wrapped around his waist. Maria got up from the chair and helped him dry off as she was pulling the towel down, she saw his dick slowly start to rise as he looked at her. She said not yet. Let's enjoy the food and then as we eat the fruit, we can get a little freaky with it. Marcus laughed because he knew those were the intentions he had, also.

As they ate the shrimp and crab cakes, Marcus and Maria talked about their future and things that they wanted to accomplish. Marcus talked about becoming a comedian one day while Maria said she would become a writer. She said what would you joke about? He said women of course. He replied what would you write about?

She said men of course. Male bashing poetry to male bashing novels and men that are cheater's. It is in their nature. Marcus said all men do not cheat, only the ones who can get away with it. Maria, chimed in "exactly" and because women work so hard and love so hard they get cheated on the most. Marcus laughed and said not true. Maria said always. I have learned that love don't love no body. Marcus said bad phrase, love always loves somebody.

They both laughed and watched a TV show while they ate the rest of the shrimp. After about an hour, they started to focus on the fruit, Marcus grabbed a strawberry and began to lick his lips, he placed the strawberry on Maria's lips, and she licked it and took a bite. Marcus took the next strawberry and placed it in the chocolate sauce and again placed it onto Maria's lips.

This time Maria took the strawberry and licked it with her fingers in place and gave a cute little sexual look to Marcus. Marcus and Maria started kissing and Marcus took another strawberry placed it near Maria's pussy and rubbed her clit with the strawberry, and then he ate it.

Then Maria took a piece of melon, dipped it in caramel and placed it on Marcus dick and started licking it with his thickness in place. Then Marcus took a strawberry and placed it on her clit and started eating it.

As they both kept taking turns on eating fruit off of each other their fingers began to play a major role in the action. Marcus thrust his fingers inside and out of Maria's pussy, and she rubbed his dick over and over with strong anticipation of penetration.

They started moaning and kissing and feeling and touching, and then Maria sat on Marcus face as he began sucking and licking her pussy as her juices flowed down Marcus face, Maria began to bend over as she saw Marcus big dick rise more and more to the occasion, she started sucking and licking his thickness, as Marcus was still sucking and tasting her liquids, as they enjoyed the taste of each other,

Maria turned around and started sucking Marcus harder and harder, then Marcus lifted Maria and sat her on his thickness, as her body got wetter and wetter, Maria felt Marcus dick penetrate her walls and it was such a beautiful feeling of thrust inside her, the deeper and deeper Marcus went Maria grabbed his shoulders and began to hold on tighter as she thrust back and forth on Marcus dick,

Marcus was moaning and his toes were curling because the wetness of Maria on his body felt so warm. Maria kept riding and moaning as the thrust became harder and harder from both of them. As they both reached a climax, they both got louder and louder with each thrust until they screamed out each other name at the same time, with pure satisfaction from one another. As they lay there next to each other,

Maria was satisfied and so was Marcus, they both knew that it was the beginning to a long -lasting relationship. About twenty minutes went by and then Maria and Marcus were back at it again. Marcus turned Maria on her stomach and began to lick her from the back, as his tongue went from the top of her neck to the crack of her ass, she knew that it was again about to be on.

He took a melon and placed the fruit at the tip of her ass and then licked her back up and down and placed the fruit in her pussy and began to eat it. Maria was taken away; she had had sex before but never had a man explore her in this way.

Maria was enjoying every bit of it. The attention, the emotion, the passion it all was there like she never knew. This man had made her reach a climax she never thought she had. The beauty of it was remarkable. After licking Maria up and down her back and ass, Marcus gently turned her over again and began to work his magic.

He took one breast in his hand and softly caressed it while licking and sucking the other breast hard and vigorous, this man must have watched porn to be so dam seductive and good at what he was doing, Maria thought quietly.

He then started to lick down her stomach and then to her clit and inside her pussy, he began to lick and suck and place his fingers near her ass hole, as he sucked her pussy, he began to rub his finger around her ass slowly, until he placed his tongue quickly around her ass while finger fucking her at this point, Maria's body was excited and ready for Marcus to fuck her hard.

As she laid there, he began to make the journey into her pussy with his big thick dick, as it plunged into her pussy she moaned with satisfaction, she began to move around in a circle motion so that Marcus could feel all of her sexual walls. She was grabbing his back and pulling him in deeper and deeper.

As he thrust his dick harder and harder into her pussy feeling every bit of satisfaction that it had to offer. Marcus and Maria went for awhile enjoying the pleasure of one another, until they again exploded with each others juices and the warmth on each others body. They lay in each others arms and went fast asleep.

When they awoke in the morning, Marcus had room service deliver them the most beautiful breakfast, French toast, with peaches, and whipped cream, bacon and eggs with sausage, and syrup. Maria was delighted, she loved being pampered and spoiled by her now "Boo".

CHAPTER FOUR

"Happy Birthday"

Maria was so happy, her and Marcus were now a couple, and was headed for the serious work that would have to be put into a relationship. Yes! things were moving fast but when you are in love who cares how fast it's moving. Maria and Marcus were happy and that was all that mattered. After that week-end Maria and Marcus spent so much time together.

Marcus was at Maria's apartment every day & night. The only other step was a door key. Maria debated over it at first, because she thought about Eric and didn't want him to get hurt.

When people enter relationships, it is really the children who miss out if it doesn't work out, because then they have become attached to a person they may never see again if it doesn't work out. Maria decided that it was time for Marcus to have a key and by this time it was Marcus birthday and Maria was ready.

As Marcus birthday got near Maria had a key made. Maria and Eric made a cake and Maria had ordered some Chinese food to celebrate the occasion. After all Marcus birthday fell on Maria's weekend with Eric so she really didn't want to plan a night out.

After decorating the cake Maria called Marcus to make sure he was going to be around for his birthday she didn't want to assume that his friends weren't going to take him out to some crazy strip club or something like that.

Marcus confirmed that he was on his way to Maria's and that he wouldn't want to be anyplace else. Maria smiled as she continued with her plans. Maria and Eric blew up balloons around the apartment, set the table with the plates and fork setting, placed the cake in the middle and waited for Marcus.

Two hours had gone by, Eric was getting restless, Maria, went out to the phone booth to call Marcus his mom said he was not there. Just as Maria started to worry Marcus pulled up. As he got out of the car, she noticed he was a little nonchalant but quickly she got over it.

As he entered the apartment Maria and Eric yelled happy birthday Marcus, his face lit up and he acknowledged that he was happy. They sat down at the table and enjoyed shrimp egg-foo young, and chicken wings with fried rice. After dinner they sang happy birthday and gave Marcus his gifts.

The first gift was a polo shirt light blue and white second gift a bottle of polo cologne the final gift lay inside a small envelope it was the key to the apartment. Marcus was so happy when he got to that one because it meant no more waking up Maria as he would come and go. He had to be to work so early that he would normally have to wake her up so she could lock the door upon him leaving.

He was so excited at the idea of just being able to come and go. After all, by this time he was helping Maria financially so it wasn't like he would be using her or anything like that. Marcus took a shower and laid down at Maria's for the night.

When morning came, he kissed Maria's for head and locked the door as he left for work. By the time Maria and Eric got up to start their day they noticed little gifts for each of them.

Eric had a little note that read have a great day with $5.00 in it, and Maria had a card that read I love you babe have a great day see you when you get home, and she had a hundred -dollar bill in her card. Maria smiled and began her and Eric's day. It was just nice to know that Marcus thought of her having lunch and bus fare every week without a problem.

Maria still spent weekends at Marcus house when she didn't have Eric with her, and on this particular week-end Maria woke up to find Marcus had already left the house to go play basketball. He left her a note saying he went to play ball with Maurice and would be back by noon.

As Maria started down the stairs to make breakfast the phone rang at Marcus house, even though she didn't live there Marcus's mom had already given her permission to treat their home like her own. Maria answered the phone and Maurice was on the other line asking where Marcus was.

Maria responded he is not in at the moment. Can I take a message? Maurice said yes Maria can you let him know I called we were supposed to go shoot some hoops today. Maria said I will give him the message and hung up the phone.

Maria continued on to make breakfast, as she finished eating Marcus came in looking sweaty as if he just played ball. Maria kissed his cheek and asked him where he had been? He replied shooting hoops with the guys (Maurice and them)

Maria looked at him again pressed star 69 on the phone to redial Maurice since he was the last incoming call on the line. Maurice answered the phone and Maria said Hey Mo, Marcus just got in you want to holler at him to see if you are still shooting hoops today.

The look on Marcus face was priceless, Maria punched him in his face, and they began to fight, Marcus's mom and stepdad came downstairs and asked what was going on. Maria replied I can't stand a liar. Marcus said I was playing ball, Maria said yeah, I guess you were, he said I'm not lying, Maurice wasn't there,

Maria replied yeah cover up your story I'm going home. Maria grabbed her things and headed for the bus stop. Marcus stepdad said you done met the right one now. Marcus hurried to his car to meet Maria around at the bus stop to be able to drive her home.

At first, they had words and Maria would not get into the car because she wanted to know where Marcus was at for so long. He kept yelling get in the car and by the third yell she jumped into the infinity.

As she fastened her seat belt Marcus was headed towards the expressway to take her home. As they drove on 76 Maria started yelling at Marcus again about where he was at. He replied I really was playing basketball. She said bull shit Maurice called while you were gone, and he was looking for your ass too. How are you going to lie to my face?

As Marcus continued to drive Maria started throwing his cd's out the sunroof. She was so disappointed that she was just beside herself and completely out of her realm. As they got closer to Maria's apartment, she told him not to use the key at this time because she was very upset with him. Marcus let Maria get out and go into the apartment, he waited until she closed the door and then he drove off.

As Maria entered her home she sat down and started to cry because she was frustrated at the thought of Marcus lying. She was also a firm believer of a quote her mother taught her, what is done in the dark will eventually come to light, don't go look for it. It will come. Maria was a searcher if it was a lie, he was telling the truth would be found.

CHAPTER FIVE

"The Move"

As Maria showered and prepared for her day, she started looking at new apartments to relocate too. Her neighborhood was getting bad with all the drug dealers and gang banging and she really didn't want Eric so close up and personal to that lifestyle.

What did it for her was a drug sting the police set up on her block, and the guy they were setting up drove up on the sidewalk in front of Maria's apartment and she realized that had Eric been home he normally just runs out of the front door to the apartment and could have easily been struck by that vehicle that day!

Maria could not get her mind from around it. Even though she was working as an Admin Assistant she was also a bartender and had hit up one of her friend's that was dating a guy named Ron who had an empty apartment on top of him. It was a corner apartment two bedroom just right for her and Eric. The only down fall was you had to go through Eric's room to get to her room. Maria didn't date many men more less really bring them home, so she wasn't worried, about that.

Maria went to meet the landlord he ran a "credit check" and Maria was approved to move in by the end of the month.

It was October and Maria was excited about the move and was not sure about giving Marcus a key to the new place because of the lie he had told. He didn't really know Maria's feelings as far as moving but she had noticed a big change in him as far as scheduling and time and more lies so it seemed.

Marcus started using the key again about a week after their minor blow up at one another. Maria was settled in for the night and Marcus used the key and came in took a shower and climbed into bed next to Maria, she looked up at him and lay back down. As she tried to sleep Marcus had other thoughts in mind. He began to kiss Maria's neck and caress her back and rub her thighs.

Maria moaned and let him know she was ready, he softly felt her breast, and sucked and licked her nipples. His hands began to work their way down to her clit as he rubbed her clit until she was wet. When he felt the wetness, he knew it was a go. He quickly placed his fingers in her pussy and began to finger fuck her just the way she liked. He placed his head in position and began to lick and suck her pussy until her juices flowed accordingly.

After satisfaction was reached, he began to rub his big juicy dick on her clit and then he pushed his thickness deep inside of her touching all her walls to satisfaction.

Maria grabbed his back with such power pulling him closer and closer to her body, until they released pure body fluids all over each other. She lay in his arms, and they went to sleep. There was no need for a round two tonight, they were both simply relaxed.

When Maria awoke in the morning, Marcus was gone. She got ready for work and started her day. While at work she received a nice arrangement of flowers, with a note that read you are the one. She placed them on her work desk and went about her day, thinking of Marcus and knowing that he was the one too.

Maria still had not had the chance to tell Marcus that she would be moving by the end of the month. That talk would have to come in the next week or so. Maria unsure of if Marcus was still hiding anything.

As the coming week approached Maria still had a heavy heart regarding Marcus and if she would tell him about the move or just move without telling him. Maria talked it over with her brother and tried to get a man's point of view before doing anything silly. Her big brother advised her if you want to be with him tell him. If not fuck it, don't tell him. Maria decided to keep it to herself for now and see how things would play out in the up coming weeks.

Maria was just happy she could afford a new place for her and Eric and knowing it would be better than the place they were in.

Marcus continued to stay the night for the up coming weeks not realizing that Maria was in the middle of moving to a new apartment. He saw the boxes packed, and the kitchen packed up, but Maria told him she was about to exterminate because she saw a bug or two and didn't want to have any bugs in her place.

Marcus nodded in agreement and that was that. Maria thought to herself yes that was believable. As the days went on, she still was unsure about telling Marcus anything.

The following week-end Maria went over to her new apartment with Eric, and they started painting and fixing up the place. Eric saw a baby kitten in the back yard of the apartment as they were bringing in some things and he started feeding the kitten milk and then of course asked for the kitten to be his.

Maria told him if no one came for the kitten by the end of the night she would not leave it in the cold. Of course, with Maria's luck no one came for the kitten. Eric named the kitten starlight, and they kept the kitten.

By the next day, all of Maria's things were moved in thanks to her best friend and her older brother. Eric was happy to have his own room, and a new kitten. And Maria was also happy to have her own room.

Maria finally got a phone now that things were picking up for her financially. She paged Marcus pager and left her number. When he called back, he said who this? She said who you want it to be? He said stop playing who is this? Maria said I thought you knew my voice so well. He said I do babe, stop playing.

Maria started getting a little suspicious just as Marcus said again come on babe, I know it's you what you doing? Maria said nothing, where are you at? Marcus said I'm about to make a run down your way. She said "okay" come on.

Maria realized that Marcus only said babe! And she knew she had moved so he didn't know the number and it wasn't the phone booth. So, she played along with him to see if he would show up at the old apartment and then call her or text her pager when he got down there, and if he went somewhere else? Then oh well she thought. At least she would know. She said ok I will be waiting for you.

Marcus hung up and Maria hung up. About an hour had gone by. No Marcus. Maria started to wonder if there was really someone else because Marcus had not called back, and he should have been to her old apartment by now. And if he had gone to use the key of course it would not work because the locks were changed. Just as Maria was about to get in the shower the phone rang, she picked it up and said hey babe, where are you?

Marcus said how did you know? It was me, she said because this is my new number, and you are the first person I gave it too.

Marcus began to laugh and said I'm out front open the door. She said you didn't try to use your key, He said yeah but it wouldn't' work. Maria started laughing so hard, and Marcus asked what was so funny. He said come on I'm at the phone booth. She said I'm sorry I don't live there anymore. He said what?

She said I decided to move and I'm in a new place. Marcus said why didn't you tell me? She said because I wasn't sure about you at first and I didn't want to move and tell you if I decided not to be with you.

Anyway, I live at 3rd and Rubicam Street. He said where is that? She said make a right on Rockland and drive down to 3rd Street make a left on 3rd and keep coming down to Rubicam. He said ok, see you in a few.

Maria jumped in the shower and as she came out, she looked outside as Marcus was parking his car. She lit a couple of candles before going down to the door to let him in.

As Marcus entered Maria's new apartment, he said nice, nice. Maria smiled and asked if he liked it. He said I really do, it's a nice place for us he joked. Maria said yeah ok, with another smile on her face.

As she showed Marcus around the apartment, he said we must sexualize every room. Maria said no not Eric's room smarty. Marcus laughed and said yes, your right every room but his.

Maria asked Marcus was he hungry, and he said yes. Maria quickly made some sea food alfredo with a side of veggies. Marcus loved Maria's cooking and he didn't have a problem with drinking kool-aid one of Maria's personal favorites. As they sat down to eat Eric was telling Marcus about the kitten he had found outside in the yard and the promise that his mom had made to him, if no one claimed the kitten.

They all laughed and continued to finish up their food. After dinner, Marcus helped Eric with some reading and Maria cleaned up the dishes. She put Eric to bed and then her and Marcus relaxed in the living-room with the candles lit and just talked and held each other for a while.

Marcus began to ask Maria about a key again when Maria already had it in her hand to give to him. As soon as Marcus got the key in his hand, he did a little funny dance and started heading to the bedroom.

He told Maria he had some of his uniforms in his trunk and would like it if he could leave one or two at her apartment for when he would spend the night. Maria didn't have a problem with that at all.

As they got in the bedroom, Marcus began to get undressed, and Maria said you are taking a shower? right? He said yes, mam. She said I don't know where you just came from! I want to believe it was home, but you never know! He said stop it you know it's only you. Maria said yeah ok.

Marcus headed into the bathroom to take a shower. When he came out him and Maria watched a little TV and called it a night. As they slept Maria was awaken by Marcus pager. Its 3:00 in the morning, who could that be?

Morning came:

As Maria had awakened Marcus had already been up dressed and out and she heard the door open as she got up from the covers, Eric and Marcus came in the room with breakfast in bed. Maria was happy even thou she still had the 3:00 pager vibrating on her mind. She quickly dismissed it again and just ate her food.

After breakfast, Marcus had a great idea to head down Penn's landing to just chill for the day. Marcus claimed he didn't like public transportation. So, they drove down to South St, parked and walked to Penn's landing. They had ice-cream and a whole lot of fun just watching people and enjoying the day.

Maria was glad that Marcus really took an interest in Eric and her time well spent. When you are a single parent it's very hard to find a man that will really want to help out, financially, emotionally and physically.

After a wonderful day Marcus dropped Maria and Eric off home and he went to his place or so he said?

CHAPTER SIX

"Who are you?"

As Marcus drove off his pager vibrated, and he pulled out his new cell phone and made a call. "Hello" said the voice on the other line. Hey babe what are you doing? Sitting here waiting on you the voice replied. Ok hold that thought I will be right there.

Marcus pulled off the expressway and started up Girard Ave. With thoughts of Maria in his heart, but Sharon on his mind, Sharon was another young lady that Marcus was seeing. She was prepared and awaiting Marcus arrival.

She had on a towel and some slippers, and her hair was in braids, she was a thick girl, busty, and very hippy. Marcus had the key to Sharon's spot. So he just parked his car on Girard Ave in front of her door, got out and went inside. Once inside Sharon knew it was on.

She worked the 11:00pm -7:00am shift and it was about 6:30pm. As Marcus went in, he first stopped at the bathroom to freshen up because he had been out with Maria all day. He came out of the bathroom wrapped in a towel, to walk down the hall to meet up with Sharon for the night. As Sharon saw him enter, she assumed position. She lay on her stomach and began to suck her fingers.

Marcus crawled on to the bed and started kissing her neck. He started playing with her pussy from behind. He gently massaged her back and rubbed it with one hand while his fingers made sure her pussy was ready.

He began to lick her pussy from the back. As he slipped his dick up in her she let out a burst of moan uughh babe, yes, she said, Marcus whispered in her ear, did you miss me? Sharon replied yes.

As Marcus began to thrust harder and harder from the back Sharon let out sighs of relief as if she was cumming over and over again. Marcus kissed her neck some and licked her from the back again. This time he pulled his dick out and finger fucked her pussy while he placed his dick inside her ass. He said shh shh it won't hurt.

As Sharon moved around because of the discomfort she finally started to move in motion with Marcus as he fucked her in the ass. She was so excited as if she was used to this position. After Marcus released his juices, he laid there for a minute and then he rolled her over and licked her pussy some more until she came again. When Sharon was sleep Marcus gathered his clothes got up and went home.

On his drive home he realized that Maria had called his pager over ten times. As he arrived in the house, he called her and acted like he had just woken up from his sleep. Maria was very suspicious but didn't really comment on it because they had such a nice evening earlier in the day. She just said good night and hung up the phone.

Marcus took a shower and went to sleep. He awoke to his pager vibrating about an hour later. It was Sharon wondering why he had got up and left her place. Marcus told her he had to come home because he had to be at work earlier than he expected and did not realize he did not bring his uniform.

Sharon cursed him out and said you normally stay over and then get up stop home and change before work. Marcus replied with whatever Sharon calm down I will give you some money tonight when I see you. She quickly calmed down and then said OK she would see him later.

Marcus laughed and shook his head because in his mind he knew that a promise of money shuts a woman up every time, after all it has always worked with his mother. Marcus continued getting ready for work, and headed in.

Upon his arrival he was greeted by Monique who worked with him. Hey Marcus, she screamed up the hallway. You didn't return my call last night. Marcus said I was pretty busy, what's up?

Monique started to say how she enjoyed their outing last week and him buying her lunch lately at work, he said awe that's nothing serious I know you just broke up with your boyfriend and I just wanted to do something nice for you.

Monique replied I got some thing you can do to me alright! Marcus looked up and said huh? She said nothing while laughing very hard, Monique said see you later Marcus and he said OK, while smiling and walking away.

All the ladies loved Marcus and he knew it so it's not like he ever had a problem with being wanted, he took ladies out, spent money on them and fucked them well, so he was well known around the city, and maybe even abroad!

CHAPTER SEVEN

"Really"

Maria was sitting at work by 9:00 am as her cell phone rang. It was Marcus wishing her a very happy good morning. She said do you ever get any work done thru out the day silly? He said rarely. Maria was happy to hear from Marcus and sat biting on the end of her pen while continuing to talk to Marcus. She started having a flash back of making love with him.

Marcus called her name three times before Maria heard him through her daydream. Maria finally responded hello; I am sorry I have a lot of work to do. Marcus said OK I will let you go take care of that, Maria smiling while saying okay. I will see you later.

As they each hung up the phone thinking of one another, Marcus was quickly brought back to reality by Monique passing him in the Janitor room. The scent of her perfume was a recent scent he had purchased for Maria and the smell aroused him.

Monique looked at Marcus and flashed her top down quickly and showed her titties, in a lace top bra. Marcus looked to see if anyone else was around. When he noticed it wasn't he began to go over to Monique and start to tug at her bra pulling it down and sucking on her breast.

She began to respond in a sexual manner and started coming out of her uniform. Marcus quickly pulled out a condom and pulled his pants down to his knees Monique begin to suck on his dick before he placed the condom on it.

He then turned her around having her hold onto the supply cart while he thrust in and out of her, she was moaning and calling out Marcus name as they had a 5 -minute pleasure of each other. When they were done, they got dressed and went back to working.

Of course, Monique text Marcus for the rest of the night, saying how she would now love coming to work everyday just to get a good fuck, while she was there. He continued to text her saying yes it would be nice to be able to get a quickie in at work everyday. While also replying to Maria, Marcus was anxious for their plans for the evening when she got off work.

Maria was off work waiting for Marcus to pick her up, as he pulled up she was flirting with him "hey handsome" he replied yes beautiful, he got out the car to open up the passenger door for her as he always did.

She was in a nice fitting red dress with a patent leather pump and a sling bag that matched, her hair was pulled back into a ponytail and the red lip gloss she had on was popping. Marcus was proud to be out with such an amazing young lady, they headed out to dinner at a restaurant in center city.

After dinner they went down to Penn's Landing just to walk around, but then Marcus noticed a little spot off to the side that had a bench in the cut, as they went in that direction they began to kiss and hug each other then Marcus sat on the bench and Maria sat on top of him, yes they begin to get it in right there in the dark on the bench at Penn's Landing, they enjoyed each other where ever they went. They walked around a little more and then went back to Maria's place.

As they arrived, Marcus did his usual and pulled out red roses from the floor behind his seat in the car and said here you are beautiful. Maria took the roses and gave him a seductive kiss as they went into her apartment. They started taking their clothes off on the stairs as they headed straight to the bedroom to finish up the encounter that started at Penn's landing.

Maria fell to sleep and Marcus stayed with her until it was time for him to leave for work. As he got up Maria asked him if he would be back after work, and he replied yes.

As Marcus arrived at work he went to doing his normal routine in the janitor's room. He gathered the things he needed, to start cleaning the restrooms in the building. While cleaning the ladies, restroom Monique saw the cleaning sign but still went into the restroom expecting to see Marcus. When Marcus looked up from cleaning one of the stalls,

Monique grabbed his thickness to see if it was responding to her advances. Sure, enough it was rising to the occasion, and Monique began to make sure it was going to stay that way. Before they could start Marcus went and put the out of order sign up on the ladies, restroom door.

As he went back into the stall, Monique was standing in there, butt naked and ready, she had hung her uniform up in the stall, he reached for her to turn her body over the clean toilet and began to finger fuck her with two fingers she began to grab her breast and suck on them.

He pulled his pants down and sat on the toilet. Monique climbed up on top and sat on his dick. She placed her feet against the wall as Marcus began to push up and down getting a good grip with his feet flat on the floor. She moaned and scratched his back to keep a good grip so that she would not fall. He continued faster and faster she screamed at the moment of her climax, and he released his cum inside of her as he held her close given a false sense of comfort.

Monique felt like this was a turning point for her and Marcus and that they were now exclusive. Marcus gently pushed her to the side as he got up to go wash off at the sink. She followed suit and quickly put her uniform back on, and they both got back to work.

One o' clock came and Marcus was leaving work, as he hit the parking lot Monique was standing next to his car, she began to ask him what was up with them. He quickly replied wait a minute we are not an item! I like kicking it with you and things are fine the way that they are.

Monique said oh ok I just wanted to be clear because I am starting to catch feelings for you, and I noticed that you did not use a condom this time? Marcus said Hey no, I did not but you are on birth control, right? Monique said no not at all. She said hopefully nothing comes out of it. Marcus said yeah hopefully not. Marcus said Well, I will talk to you later, and he got in his car and left.

As he was driving up 76, he got a text from Sharon asking him was he on his way over, he text back yes what are you cooking us for lunch she replied cheeseburgers and chips, he said bet.

As he parked his car Sharon had his food upstairs in the room while she jumped into the shower. As Marcus entered Sharon's house with his key, he went straight upstairs to her room and noticed his food was ready and she was in the shower getting ready for him. He began to eat his food and turned the channel on the television, flicking thru several channels until he reached the porn.

Sharon came out the bathroom and started to come over to Marcus while dropping her towel. He said he had to take a shower first thinking of the earlier encounter with Monique. And he also wanted to quickly touch base with Maria to see how her day was going.

He quickly went into her bathroom turned the water on and called Maria asking how her day was going, saying how he did not have much time because he just got home and was about to jump into the shower. Maria understood and said call me later.

As Marcus exited the bathroom, he was ready for Sharon, he came to the bed climbing on top of her placing his fingers into her mouth and his tongue into her pussy. As he licked her clit and sucked her clit while fucking her with his tongue, she was moaning and grabbing his back feeling the scratches created by Monique earlier in the day. When they where finished they went to sleep cuddling with each other until Sharon had to go to work.

Marcus left her house at 9:30pm and started his way to Maria's house. When he arrived, Maria was in the shower getting ready for bed. She came out to see Marcus entering her bedroom and taking off his clothes saying he was spending the night and going to work from there. She said OK.

He picked up the remote, and turned to the porn channel, getting ready for sex with Maria, Maria looked at Marcus and said come on baby I am tired I have a long day tomorrow! I have to work and then it is parent teacher night at Eric school. Marcus understood and turned to the TV to the news as he held Maria close and just went to sleep.

CHAPTER EIGHT

"New Friends"

Marcus was getting too comfortable with the women in his life, Maria, Sharon, and Monique. Monique had hit Marcus up recently at work saying that she missed her period. Marcus was like oh ok I will talk with you later about it.

Do not come in my face with that kind of talk at work. Mean while he was still sexing her up on lunch breaks in the bathroom and the janitorial closet.

Later on, that day when he got off work Monique was waiting at his car. She said I can not have this baby Marcus. He said who else are you seeing? She angrily replied I am only fucking with you.

He laughed and put his head down while shaking it. He looked up again quickly and said listen, I have a lady you knew this, I do not understand why you do not have protection for yourself.

Monique replied well you started off using condoms! Nobody told you to stop. Marcus looked at her and said make an appointment and I will take care of it. She nodded her head and walked away.

Meanwhile Marcus shook his head again laughed and drove off. As he hit 76 he headed towards Maria's apartment and then he got a call on his cell phone from Sharon. Hello Marcus answered. Hey Marcus what's up I need to holler at you for a second, He said ok shoot. She said I have been feeling kind of funny lately, He said oh really! Let me guess you think you are pregnant?

Sharon quickly responded yes. She said you know I cannot have a baby! I do-not have time for that, I told you that last time. Marcus said I thought you told me you were on birth control. Sharon said you know that is not full proof baby, nothing is.

Marcus shook his head and said listen I will talk to you later. I need to think about something, but don't worry I will take care of it. Sharon said OK and hung up. Marcus proceeded to Maria's.

Marcus was not really a drinker, he did not smoke or do drugs, sex was his drug, and he liked porn money and fucking. Everything else was just a tease. Basketball was his down time, and he was just getting into some new hobbies more women that is.

Maurice and his boy Kevin had hit Marcus up and asked him to meet up with them at the Picka Dilly club, every body knows what that is, a place full of strippers and lap dances.

Let me describe the boys that play attire for this occasion, a loose fitting but comfortable t-shirt that does not hang to low over the waist and a medium fit light weight sweat pant.

So that as the lap dance is being performed the juices released by the stripper will wet the thin attire sweat pant and the thickness will rise to the occasion.

Marcus detoured and met up with his boys, as they entered the spot, the strippers begin to make themselves available, one by one approaching each of the men. Marcus looked interested in the Hispanic chic she introduced herself as Rose,

Rose was medium built small breast thick hips wearing a white feathered thong and two white feathered pasties over her breast.

She was licking her lips which had cherry red lip gloss and a feather in her hair to complete the attire. As Marcus glanced down and saw her red pumps, he knew there was an immediate attraction.

Rose glanced down at Marcus quickly to let him know that it was about to go down, she grabbed his hand and guided him to one of the private rooms.

Once inside Rose escorted Marcus to a comfortable chair, as she grabbed a flavored strawberry whip cream, she began to spray it on her fingers and lick them very sexually,

Marcus was excited she then took a blindfold from the front of her thong and gently tied it around his eyes, he hesitated at first, but she assured him that it would make the experience more enjoyable.

She then turned on some soft music as she began to rub a feather from her thong across his lips, she then started to lap dance on Marcus, first she took his finger and sprayed some whip cream on it as she sucked it off with her mouth,

Then she began to lick and suck his fingers even harder as she swayed her ass back and forth swiftly across his thickness, it was starting to rise because of the friction and the sucking on his fingers, as she continued to sway, she then sat completely on Marcus dick as it elevated through the sweatpants.

Rose could feel the hardness as she swayed and rubbed on it back and forth, her juices started to release, Marcus began to moan and say don't stop, Rose wasn't planning to. She began to place his fingers on the front of her thong towards her clit.

He began to rub it on his own while massaging her breast a little with the other hand. Against the rules Marcus placed his fingers into Rose's pussy and was finger fucking her hard, She, didn't stop him Instead she removed his blindfold, so she could look into his eyes.

As she starred at him, he began to pull his sweatpants down just enough to expose his nice sized hard dick, Rose started to pull her thong to the side she moaned loudly as Marcus thickness entered her body, she rode it harder and harder until Marcus burst out a loud oh my lawd.

She continued riding him harder until he grabbed her breast harder, and he released his pleasure and energy all up inside of her, as she got up off of him Marcus was reaching in his wallet to pay her for her services, He opened her hand and placed two hundred dollars in it.

Rose looked at him as if she was ashamed and then she said I only do this to help me pay for school, Marcus responded I'm not judging you. Rose replied I don't normally fuck my clients just give them a regular lap dance.

Marcus said OK! Well, I am a client. Rose said yes, I know, but I liked you so I decided that you would become more than a client. Marcus smiled and said what nights do you work? Rose said Wednesday, Friday and Sunday. He said I will be back to see you; He gave her his pager number cleaned himself up and was ready to roll.

Meanwhile Maurice and Kevin were already out in the lobby waiting. As Marcus emerged out of the room, they both looked at him and said dam man what took you so long? Marcus shrugged his shoulders and replied with a smirk on his face (it was a great session) you know!

Maurice and Kevin shook their heads and started laughing as they all exited the Dilly. Marcus said yo! I'm going to hit yawl up later this week, I'm heading to Maria's for the night they shook hands, and each drove their separate ways.

CHAPTER NINE

"The Craziness"

Maria was in the kitchen cleaning up as Marcus entered the apartment with his key. He quickly walked over to her and gave her a kiss. She turned away and said you were supposed to be here over an hour ago. Marcus looked at her and said I had to make a quick stop. She said OK well you could have called. He responded why I was still coming.

Maria said stop getting smart, he said I'm not getting smart I'm just saying that I had to make a quick stop and I'm here now, Maria was still upset as she explained to Marcus that it was past 11:00pm and she didn't appreciate him coming over so late like this was about to be a booty call. Marcus said we aren't even fucking tonight. Ok Maria said Okay.

Eric jumped up out of bed because he heard Marcus and his mom talking, he ran in the kitchen given Marcus a huge hug, and asked him when they were hanging out again, Marcus said this weekend little man, Maria intervened and said OK Eric time for you to get back in bed, He said awe man, as he hugged Marcus one more time and headed back in his room.

Marcus said why do you have to be so hard on him she replied I'm not you are the one that is late getting here. Come earlier and maybe I will believe that you are getting serious about this relationship, Marcus laughed and said I am serious about this relationship.

He then jumped into the shower and came out and started watching porn, Maria said darn it Marcus, stop watching porn, what are you addicted, to this shit. Marcus laughed and said no I'm addicted to you as he started trying to hug and kiss Maria, she quickly pushed him off of her and said stop baby, I'm tired.

Morning came and Marcus was already gone as Maria and Eric opened their eyes and got their day started, as normal, Marcus left $10.00 for Eric and a hundred dollars for Maria, they both started doing a happy dance as they left out the door.

Eric wanted to go to the store before Maria dropped him at the daycare, they went into the store and Eric bought Doritos and popcorn and a hug juice, Maria made him pay for it out of his money and then she took the rest to put up for another day.

After dropping Eric at daycare, Maria continued on to work, as she got there, she started having a headache she thought maybe due to her rushing this morning after dropping Eric off.

She drank a glass of water and then proceeded to continue working throughout the day. Marcus called her on his break, Maria took her break an explained to him how bad she felt, but she was going to still try to get thru the day.

Marcus said he would pick up Eric and she could go straight home, and he would meet her at the apartment later with dinner. Maria agreed and said she would see him then.

As Maria came thru the door, she began to feel worse and worse and everything possible was running through her mind, from pregnancy to STD, to health issues and etc.

She sat down on the side of her bed and started to feel dizzy, she called Marcus who got to her in 15 minutes from across the city, he carried her to the car and rushed her over to Jean's hospital where she was seen and diagnosed with dehydration.

Maria hadn't been drinking enough fluids and she was always so busy between work and caring for Eric and of course getting it in with Marcus.

When Maria and Marcus arrived back at the apartment Marcus, went to dunkin donuts and got Maria some tea with lemon and picked up some bottles of water for her to consume throughout the night. He also picked up Eric on his way back in and told Eric to be very good because mommy was very tired and needed to rest.

Eric shook his head and took the opportunity to ask Marcus could they stop at Game Stop and pick up a new game, so that's where they went before heading back in.

Eric ran through the apartment door straight over to Maria and said mom feel better I'm going to play my new game. Marcus laughed and said yeah baby I picked him up a new game so he could play that instead of bothering you.

He handed Maria her tea kissed her on her lips and told her to get some rest. She hugged him and said okay. Marcus told her he had to make a few runs and he would be back later to spend the night. Maria replied" you have your key, right? He said of course.

As Maria lay on her bed comfortably, she couldn't help but wonder why Marcus had left instead of hanging around with her for a little while longer, she picked up her phone and called her best friend Lacy and begin to tell her the story of the day. Lacy said thank heaven he rushed you to the hospital, and you are ok.

Maria told her he had left and said he would return later, Lacy said girl don't worry about that man, he pays your bills, he is nice to you and Eric, and he loves you that's all that really matters. Maria said yeah! I guess so, and they hung up so Maria could rest.

About four hours had past and Marcus had returned with dinner for Maria and Eric as he had promised. They sat at the table ate dinner and all retired to bed.

The next morning Marcus had left early for work, Maria was feeling better and got herself and Eric together quickly to start their day, as usual Marcus left $10.00 dollars for Eric and $100.00 dollars for Maria and they both did their thank you dance out of the apartment door.

CHAPTER TEN

"A wandering mind"

Maria and Eric arrived home and Marcus was already in the Apartment, as Eric ran to the bedroom door, Marcus was like whoa, whoa, I'm not dressed lil man. Maria quickly intervened and said Well why not? Marcus explained that he had come over right from work because he wanted to surprise her and Eric. Dinner was on the stove and there were roses in the vase on the table.

Maria smiled and began to set the table. Eric ran to let Marcus know that dinner was being served. Marcus came out of the room with sweatpants and no shirt on. Maria was quickly drawn to what looked like a passion mark on Marcus left shoulder,

As she sat down next to him at the table, she said Hey baby what is this? A burn or something? Marcus said no that's just a bruise from basketball with the guys, here you go. Maria said oh I was just wondering.

After dinner they all sat down and watched a family movie, Marcus went into the kitchen and pulled out some popcorn from the cabinet and began to pour it into a bowl so they all could really feel like they were at the movies.

While sitting next to Maria, she felt the vibration of Marcus's cell phone buzzing. He pulled it out and said it was nobody. It continued to vibrate so clearly it was someone that felt it was important enough to keep calling back.

Maria just brushed it off and continued to cuddle with Marcus and watch the movie, not wanting to spoil the night for Eric and Maria. When the movie was over Maria put Eric down to bed and thought that her and Marcus would be going to bed as well.

Marcus started putting on his shirt and sneakers, as he came out of the room telling Maria he had to leave, and he probably wouldn't be back tonight because he had to be at work and wanted to get a good rest at home in his own bed.

Maria said ok and just turned her head as he tried to kiss her on her lips. She said just get out playboy, He said never that I don't have time I'm always working and playing ball. Marcus left out of the door and Maria sat there wondering and praying that Marcus wasn't cheating on her.

Maria jumped into the shower and just sat back and cleared her mind, wanting to wash any thoughts of Marcus cheating on her down the drain.

As she emerged from the shower and wrapped into a towel she headed towards her bedroom and as she sat on the bed her cell phone began to ring it was her best friend, Lacy. Lacy was just checking on Maria to see if she had been feeling better since the hospital episode.

Maria explained that she was feeling much better and that she was just about to turn in for the night, Lacy told her to rest well, and she would talk to her later.

Maria was glad she didn't bring up the fact that she felt deep in her gut that she was being cheated on. She just didn't want to worry Lacy and get Lacy into speaking negative about Marcus.

She knew that she didn't want to revisit that thought with Lacy until she was sure that there was some negative thought to visit.
Maria turned off the TV and she went to bed.

Meanwhile across town, Marcus was just getting started. He was returning Rose's call from the Picka Dilly, Rose answered quickly and let Marcus know that she was about to start her shift. He said okay, I am on my way.

While in route, Marcus called Maurice and Kevin, to let them know he was heading over to the Picka Dilly. They said bet we will meet you there, As Marcus walked thru the doors Rose was at the booth waiting for him.

She had on royal blue sequence thongs and some matching sequence pasties that covered most of her nipples. Accompanied by some silver high heel shoes with sequence.

As Rose starred at Marcus he immediately began to respond and rubbed the front of his sweatpants while licking his lips in anticipation of what he knew was about to go down.

Rose grabbed Marcus hand and slowly guided him to the royal room where she would be for the night. Marcus told her he wanted to pay for two sessions tonight. Rose eyes lifted as she smiled, because she knew she was going to get a nice pay this evening.

As she guided him to the chair and began to get him comfortable Marcus grabbed her hand and guided her to the couch. He said he wanted a different vibe tonight. He laid Rose on the couch and began to lick up and down her entire body.

He spread her legs opened as he licked in between each thigh and worked his way deeper towards her pussy. He licked and twirled his tongue around her inner thigh slowly, he then thrust his tongue into her vagina while placing his finger into her asshole.

She began to move and moaned that hurt, he said it will feel good in a minute, he went from one finger to two in her ass trying to prepare it for what he was about to do. Rose said I have never tried it in the back, Marcus said just relax I got this.

He continued to lick and suck her pussy, she said don't stop. He came up for a minute to slide out of his sweatpants and prepare his dick for entry to her ass. He lifted her legs up and placed them gently on his forearms.

He played with her asshole with his dick first poking at it like it was a sword. Finally, it was wet enough to be caught and gripped up by the tenderness of her ass hole.

He began to thrust in and out softly as Rose began to get adjusted and started to intake the pressure from his hard thickness inside of her. Marcus said just relax and it will start to feel good,

She relaxed as he continued to gently moan and go in and out of her while enjoying pure pleasure. He continued as she moaned, and he moaned until they both released their juices onto one another.

He lay on top of her and just lapse for a minute. He then began to suck slowly on her breast until her vagina started to contract and prepare for his entry. He grabbed her hand and started to suck on her fingers while placing his fingers inside of her pussy and going in and out.

Rose began to lick her lips and move her body in a circular motion, Marcus lifted her back up a little and then he placed her legs on each shoulder so that he could go as deep as he could inside of her.

Rose began to grab his back so that she could have a good grip as he began to put his thickness deep inside of her. They began to do it until they released and released again, Marcus dick stayed hard for Rose, and she knew that was a good thing,

After they were done, Marcus cleaned himself off and placed $500.00 dollars into Rose hand kissed her cheek and then left.
As she tried to go after him, he turned to her and said let it be what it is. And then he closed the door.

CHAPTER ELEVEN

"Clearing up one mess"

Marcus headed home after talking with Maurice and Kevin outside of the Picka Dilly, as he walked thru his door his mother said someone name Kaye, came by here for you. Marcus said okay and started his way up stairs to his room.

As he turned the shower on in the bathroom, he called Maria to be sure to say good night. Rose had left a message saying how she enjoyed the sexual session and she hoped that this was the beginning of something good, especially since Marcus was beginning to pay her very well for their sessions and she had bills to pay so she was more than willing to continue fucking him.

Mean while the next morning Marcus had to meet Monique at an abortion clinic at Park Ave. and Tabor Road. When he got off the elevator on the second floor he walked up to the front desk and asked was Monique in the back yet. The receptionist said no, she hasn't arrived yet.

Just as Marcus was about to take a seat Monique came through the door. She was rushing and looked flushed. Marcus asked her was she okay, she replied yes and continued to the receptionist desk.

Hello! my name is Monique I have an 8:00am appointment the receptionist asked her to please take a seat and she would be right with her. Monique sat next to Marcus as they started to talk about the procedure.

Marcus asked her was she sure she wanted to do this. She explained yes and how she didn't want to be walking around with a baby not conceived out of love but lust.

The receptionist called out Monique name and handed her some information sheets that needed to be filled out. They had questions about her prior history and how many children and STD's she has had along with some questions on if she was allergic to any medicines or foods etc.

Marcus was curious and tried to reach over to see the paperwork, Monique said this is none of your business. He said okay but damn I have been fucking you raw what do you mean it's not my business?

Monique got up and handed the information back to the receptionist and waited to be called. About five minutes went by and she was called back up to the front to make payment.

The receptionist said that will be $300.00 Marcus stood up and pulled the money from his wallet, after he paid about five minutes later Monique was called to the back. Marcus was not allowed in the back to witness the procedure.

About a half and hour had past and Marcus was getting nervous pacing back and forth wondering if she would go thru with the procedure. She came out of the back with a prescription in her hand and some paperwork providing instructions.

Marcus hugged her and told her she would be ok. She had tears in her eyes and told Marcus she was sorry that she had done this. Marcus said no it's fine it was really the best decision she had made. They started walking to the elevator to go downstairs to the pharmacy that was right outside the building to get her prescription filled.

After that Marcus drove Monique to her house and walked her up to her front door. She dug into her purse and pulled out her key and gave it to him. Marcus unlocked the door and let her in as he began to tell her that he was not going to stay. He said he felt she needed to be alone at this time after such a procedure.

Monique looked at him with tears in her eyes and said this was your baby too you mutha fucka, He said I know you told me. But I really have to go I have to make it to work by 3:00 today I will try and stop back by when I get off to see if you need anything.

Marcus was pulling off and headed to work as his cellphone started to ring. It was Sharon saying that she had scheduled an appointment for an abortion. She was really blunt with it and requested the $400.00 dollars that she claimed it was going to cost.

She said she was 12 weeks pregnant and that she had to hurry up and have it done, Marcus assured her that he would swing by this evening and give her the money. She said ok I will see you later he said sure.

Marcus continued on his way in to work, as he arrived, he over- heard, his supervisor say that Monique was on her last leg in the office she had called out and requested the next day off too.

He shook his head while walking by saying damn man, give her a break, some women have it harder than us dealing with kids and shit. The supervisor responded by saying yeah okay you want to be right behind her. She is going on warning.

CHAPTER TWELEVE

"Clearing up the next mess"

Three o'clock came and Marcus was clocking out when he got a call from Monique asking him if he could swing by and bring her some hot tea and something to eat. Marcus told her he would be by in a little.

He pulled out from the parking garage at his job and headed home. As he arrived at his door, he noticed Kaye coming down his steps and heading his way. Kaye was a girl from the neighborhood that he had met when she moved back around the corner from his house on 60th street He was driving by one day and saw her walking from the bus stop. Followed her and got her number.

Kaye was light-skinned small framed big breast, short hair cut and light brown eyes she was a good looking, lady with a shy timid voice. As she approached the car Marcus rolled down the window, hey pretty lady he said, what's up with you?

She replied nothing much it's only my third time around here this week, you are never home. Marcus replied and said well I am now. Kaye said well what's up you want to go to the movies or grab something to eat?

Marcus said sure just give me about an hour I have to make a run, I will swing by and pick you up then so be ready. Kaye said sure I will be ready in an hour.

Marcus ran in the house to change his clothes right quick and then hurried out to get tea and something to eat for Monique, as he pulled up to her house, he saw a man coming down her steps he waited until he got in his car and pulled off and then he parked and knocked on the door, Monique said who is it and he said Marcus.

The door is un-locked, and Marcus entered, Monique was walking slowly and sat down on her couch in the living-room, Marcus handed her the tea and a sandwich he had picked up for her. She said thank you and stood up to give him a hug. She tried to tell him how sorry she was for doing what she had done, He said it's fine Monique you did what you had to do for your life.

He kissed her on her forehead and said let me know if you need anything, as he turned and walked towards the door, she said is it over is this it for us, Marcus said just worry about getting better and going back to work as soon as you can. Monique put her head down in shame and Marcus said listen it is going to be okay.

He left out the door, got in his car and drove off towards Sharon's house. As he arrived, he pulled out his key and walked in, Sharon was upstairs talking on the phone confirming an appointment at the clinic for tomorrow. Marcus overheard the scheduling and she hung up the phone he said I won't be able to go with you I have to work tomorrow.

Sharon bust out laughing and said I don't need you to go with me, I will be fine, I just need the money to pay for it because I'm not. Marcus reached into his wallet and pulled out the $400.00 dollars and placed it into Sharon hand. She said thank you and I hope you understand that I have to do this I just can't have no baby right now.

Marcus looked at her and said you have to do what you have to do I can't stop you as long as you get it done. Sharon said yes, I just can't have a baby right now even though it would be a beautiful baby I just can't I am struggling my ass off and I work nights and? Well, you know.

Marcus asked Sharon to call him as soon as she gets home tomorrow, and he would bring her something to eat when he got off work.

Sharon said she would do that and walked
Marcus to the door, Marcus kissed her on her cheek,
walked to his car and pulled off.

As Sharon closed her door, she started recounting
the money that Marcus had given her, and laughing
loud hysterically, she said yeah dummy I'm going
shopping tomorrow, thank you very much.

She called her girlfriend Tanya and said girl men
are so stupid but I'm glad because I needed this
little shopping spree.

Tanya laughed and said you got him with the
abortion game again? Girl how many times the man
going to believe that dumb shit.

Hey as many times as he falls for it. I'm going to
play him. If he wants to be my bank, I'm going to
let him.

Tanya said Sharon you crazy, Sharon said yes, I am
girl.

Marcus arrived outside of Kaye's house to pick her up. She heard him pull up and made her way outside to the car, she hopped in and started joking with Marcus, about what movie they were about to go see. Marcus said shut up before we go make our own movie. They both laughed as they headed to the 69th street theater.

As they arrived the movie was about to begin Kaye sat down and Marcus headed to get the popcorn and some drinks, He looked down and noticed that Maria had called him twice, he continued to get the snacks and drink and headed back to the movie and sat next to Kaye, the movie started.

After the movie Kaye and Marcus went down to Penn's Landing to walk around and enjoy the evening, he placed his arm around Kaye, and they walked and talked about future plans of being together. Marcus said maybe you will be the one you have no kids, a good job and me. They laughed and enjoyed the evening.

Marcus dropped Kaye off at home walked her to her door kissed her cheek and left. As he drove off Kaye was thinking of how they had such a beautiful night and how she couldn't wait to see Marcus again.

Marcus pulled up in front of his door got out and went inside up the stairs and to his waterbed. He thought of Kaye and touched base with Maria leaving her a voicemail on her phone saying that he just woke up and that he would be down there in an hour.

CHAPTER THIRTEEN

"The Lies Become Real"

The morning came and Maria realized that Marcus did not come as promised in his message she decided not to call him at all that day nor accept his call. As she suspected the calls had begun. Her phone was going off with messages from Marcus asking why she was not picking up the phone.

Maria got her and Eric ready and started out their day. Marcus called Maria's job three times before she arrived in. Maria's supervisor had let her know that Marcus had called and a reminder of no personal phone calls, Maria said yes sir as she hurried through the office and clocked in.

Her cell phone was steady ringing, finally she answered. Yes Marcus. What do you want? He said just listen to me, she said I am at work, and you are such a liar, he began to try and explain that he fell asleep last night and that's why he didn't show up.

Maria quickly replied "whatever" you are and have been acting very funny lately and I am not feeling it. Marcus said baby please don't be like this, I will be over there today. Maria said okay so she could get him off of her line and get back to work. They hung up and Maria got back to work, she felt very frustrated for the rest of the day.

Marcus was at work also and he contacted Sharon to see if she had gone to have the procedure done. She answered her phone and told Marcus that she was just arriving to the clinic on Lancaster Ave, and she would call him back once the procedure was completed.

Marcus said okay and told her that he would be by later to bring her something to eat and to please let him know if she needed anything else. Sharon said yes sure I will keep you posted.

Sharon hung up and continued on her way to the King of Prussia mall to go shopping. She was so happy that she was spending Marcus money instead of hers, Sharon went from store to store buying outfits and picking up sneakers and shoes her favorite things.

Marcus called Sharon again a couple of hours later she was on her way back from the mall, she said let me call you back in a very sleepy voice, he said I am stopping over in a few, she said no I am resting I will call you later.

Marcus got off work and made his way down to Maria's apartment she was not home yet, but he knew he had work to do. He picked up some roses and dinner and took it in the apartment. He left a card that said I love you and I can't live without you.

By the time Maria got in with Eric she noticed the Roses and card and the dinner on top of the stove it was still warm. So, she knew Marcus had just left. She didn't call his cellphone to say thank you because she knew he would be back.

As she guessed Marcus was back in about an hour, he had little gifts for her and Eric, along with dessert. Eric was happy with his gift and ran to his room to start playing with it. Maria on the other hand was not so easily flattered, by her gold chain and bracelet.

She said sit down Marcus we need to talk. Marcus sat beside her and said what is it? Maria began to tell him how she felt about the last couple of days and the way Marcus had been acting.

Marcus assured Maria that there was nothing going on and that she had nothing to worry about, Maria began to laugh and said you better be serious Marcus I don't have time for no games, I could be with someone that really loves me and will not think twice about being faithful to me.

Marcus smiled and said I understand baby and don't worry I'm going to show you how much I love you. Maria said yeah you do that. They sat up and watched a movie and then went to bed.

Morning came and Marcus was off to work first, and as usual Eric got $10.00, and Maria had $100.00 dollars and they did their little happy dance out the door and started their day.

Marcus got to work and started his day as he looked up by the time clock stood Monique, she was back to work from having the abortion, she looked at Marcus and said I know you got lunch, right?

Marcus shook his head and just walked away from Monique, as he kept walking, she was yelling out I know you don't want me to tell anybody about this lil situation right here.

He said what situation she said the abortion got to pay if you don't want to be exposed. Marcus shook his head again and just kept walking to the janitor's room.

Once inside he called Maria to say good morning, she answered the phone and said good morning to you too baby I can't wait to see you later I have a lil surprise for you. He said really? she said really. He said oh well I can't wait. They hung up happy

He then called Kaye, Good morning baby Kaye said, Marcus said hey baby just calling to see how your morning is going, she said it's fine now that you are on the other line. He said like wise. She said will I see you later Marcus said I'm not sure right now, but I will let you know as the day moves along.

Kaye said okay baby, don't do anything I wouldn't do. He said you either and, by the way did you get a delivery at work yet, she said that was you awe thank you so much the roses are beautiful. Marcus said you are so welcome, smell them and think of me, Kaye replied all day everyday baby.

Marcus got off work and swung straight by Sharon's house she opened the door as he turned his key, she said what do you want? He said I am checking to make sure you are okay after having the procedure; she said I am fine Marcus.

Marcus started walking around the house and looking into rooms, Sharon said what are you doing silly you have a key who am I going to have over here? Marcus laughed and said you would be surprised what some women do?

Sharon said Well, how long have you known me? Exactly I am not one of those women. Marcus laughed and started to make his way towards the door, Sharon remembered that she couldn't have sex and she really didn't have an abortion, so she had better let Marcus leave.

Marcus turned to her kissed her cheek and said baby make sure you feel better and call me if you need me. Sharon said yes baby I will.

CHAPTER FOURTEEN

"More Lies Come to Light"

Marcus arrived home to find Kaye knocking on his door, she noticed him pulling up. He looked down at his phone and realized Maria had been calling him because he was supposed to be coming over there.

Kaye was looking at him through the windows and he hadn't rolled one down yet. Kaye looked at him with an attitude and Marcus was trying to call Maria right quick but couldn't, so he continued to park the car and got out.

Kaye said no window, huh? Marcus said I was parking she said yes and normally you roll down the window and talk to me while you are parking?

Marcus walked towards Kaye and kissed her and said you are coming inside? She replied yes why not. They went in and walked up the stairs to Marcus room, Kaye sat down on the waterbed, and said this feels nice.

Marcus said why don't you get undressed and lay down and feel the waves. Kaye said okay. Guess that means I'm hanging out for a while.

Marcus jumped into the shower right quick before getting into his bed with Kaye. As they lay there Marcus begin flicking the remote looking for the porn channel, Kaye looked at him and said this isn't a movie he said I know we are about to watch and learn some things, he had a smirk on his face while he turned her on her side, and he observed her body.

Kaye begins to get comfortable the more Marcus begin to talk about how beautiful her breast were and how her stomach had a belly ring that he could lick in anticipation of going further down to make her feel real good.

As Marcus landed on the porn channel, he wanted he began to lick his lips and gaze more at Kaye's soft breast and ass. He reached over and started to lick slowly on her ear while placing his fingers near her pussy,

As he began to push his fingers inside of her and felt her wetness, as he pulled them out, he knew she was ready, he continued to lick her ear around to her neck as he made his way to the left side of her breast, he put her nipple inside of his mouth and began to suck it like a bottle.

Kaye began to get more and more aroused by his actions her body was yearning for his dick to be inside of her. As he continued to suck on her breast she began to whisper come get it into his ear, ,

Marcus thickness began to rise, and he was ready to see how Kaye felt inside, he licked and sucked on her belly button where a piercing was and eventually made his was down to her pussy.

As he licked and sucked her clit she moaned and squirmed to let him know she was ready for entry. Marcus sucked and sucked her clit until he felt her release a wet wonder, as he prepared for entry into her thick wet smooth pussy she gasped as the thickness entered her body.

It was like a perfect fit of togetherness she began to move her body along with his to get a better grip. As they continued in circular motion Kaye began to scream right there oh right there.

Marcus said yes yes tell me again where, Kaye said ohh right there, don' t stop, as Marcus continued he was thrusting his dick in and out harder and harder, she was screaming at the top of her lungs,

Marcus placed one of his fingers into her mouth for her to suck on she was sucking so hard and moving her body with his, that they both reached a pleasant climax and just lay into each other arms.

Marcus was not done, he took his finger and started rubbing her cum near her ass so that it would be wetter, and he also wanted to see if she was down with it.

As he rubbed on her ass and then slid his first finger inside while sucking on her breast, she began to slowly go into motion with him. He knew she was down.

He continued sucking on her breast a little while longer than he assumed her into position, turning her slightly on her stomach so his entry would be easier.

Marcus grabbed her breast while he lay behind her and started to slowly enter her ass from the back.

Kaye gasped at first and clinched up tight, Marcus said relax baby just relax and give me that ass, I will make it feel so good just trust me.

Kaye started to unwind as Marcus continued to softly whisper in her ear while he put his fingers into her pussy while continuing to fuck her softly in her ass.

She began to move with him in motion until they both released their juices, and he was done, he rolled over and just lay there accomplishing another pussy and ass award for his collection.

About an hour had passed, Marcus jumped up at the sound of his cell phone, and it was Maria calling to find out what time he would be there. He jumped up and went into the bathroom to take the call. He said hey baby, Maria said hey, what time are you coming? Marcus said I will there in about an hour. Maria said see you then.

Marcus got back into bed with Kaye and told her that he had to be somewhere with Maurice in an hour, Kaye said give me five more minutes, Marcus said I will drop you around the corner on my way out.

Ten minutes passed and Marcus got up and started getting ready, Kaye got up and asked if she could wash off, Marcus said you are only going around the corner. She said ok but dam I don't want my sister to smell me. He said ok but make it quick my mom is home,

They both got dressed, Marcus drove Kaye and dropped her off around the corner and he hurried up to get to Maria, as he turned the key to the door, he smelled the scent of candles and food, a combination he truly loved.

Maria came out of the room and said I thought I heard some noise! Marcus greeted her with a kiss and said what do we have here? Maria laughed and said I just wanted to surprise you with a little something after all you are always being so nice to Eric and me.

As she opened the door Marcus saw that the table was set for two with the candles lit and a home cooked meal, Maria had prepared a three -course meal; appetizer was fried shrimp and crab balls, main dish baked Cornish hens, sweet potatoes and spinach, and to top it off a chocolate cake.

Marcus eyes lit up with excitement and he was hungry. As they sat down Maria asked him how his day was and told him all about hers. The candles scent of roses filled the air in the apartment and as they finished up with dinner, they sat on the couch because they were stuffed.

Marcus said wow we always go out or I bring take out this was the best meal I have had in a very long time. He reached over and kissed Maria on her lips and said thank you that was delicious baby. Maria was blushing happily and on cloud nine,

Marcus said baby now we can sit back chill and watch a movie, but first let me jump into the shower and then it's a wrap, Maria said well while you are doing that let me clean up this kitchen and then I will join you in the bedroom.

Maria got started in the kitchen and Marcus was in the shower, Maria finished up first and noticed Marcus cell phone vibrating on the couch, she picked it up and took it to him but not before glancing at the incoming call.

It read Kaye, Maria opened the bathroom door and said your phone is ringing, Marcus took it from her quickly and said oh this is my cousin Kaye I will call her back later.

Maria went back into the kitchen and felt that feeling in your gut that implies some thing is up and that call was not from Marcus's cousin.

Maria started to question Marcus about the phone call but then she humbled herself and thought she should lay low and wait to find out more before jumping to conclusions. Everything was fine between the two of them no need in ruffling feathers right now.

Maria came back into the room by this time Marcus was already in the bed reminding her that the dinner was so delicious; Maria nodded her head in agreement and started watching the movie that was on the TV.

Marcus fell fast asleep, as Maria was deep in thought throughout the night about that phone call. Reality was setting in and she was just really wondering about Marcus on a different level. As he snored through the night Maria tossed and turned and got no sleep.

Morning came quickly for Marcus he jumped up got dressed kissed Maria and ran out the door to work. Maria dragged herself out of the bed, got dressed and danced out the door with the $100.00 dollars Marcus had left her.

She was off from work, so she decided to visit her best friend Lacy, as she arrived at Lacy house, she rang the bell only to find that Lacy had already gone out for the day.

Maria ended up at the Cheltenham mall and having breakfast at a small cafe not to far from the mall. Later that day Lacy had called her to say she was heading over to Maria's apartment. Maria said I will meet you there.

As Maria arrived Lacy was pulling up, what's up girl, what's going on? Maria said wait until I tell you. They went inside and Maria began to explain she started off about dinner Marcus in the shower and the phone call.

Lacy told her to just relax, you already know men are dogs girl, why would you expect any different, I'm not saying be disrespected but you have to do your homework and see what you are working with.

First find out if he is a playboy or a husband and the only way to find out is to be patient, stay focused and just play your part.

Start making him take you out more and start seeing if he invites you over to his mom's house more or if he is fading off from that.

Maria agreed with Lacy and said bet it' s on, I
am going to find out. I need to be serious about my
life; I have Eric to think about. It is not just me
anymore, and even though Marcus is good with my
son if he is cheating on me I don' t want any parts
of being second best.

Lacy agreed and told her just relax and lay low
girl things will be fine. I went through the same
bullshit with Keith remember how long before I
found out he was dropping that girl off on his way
home from work? I drove him to work and picked
him up, I dared that bitch to ask him for a ride. I
was waiting too.

I was going to punch her lights out, good thing I
am not like that anymore saved and worry free
"thank you Jesus" God will let you know if he is
the one or not so do not worry,

As Lacy and Maria continued talking and
gathering thoughts of prediction for Maria's future,
Lacy reminded her that nothing in life is free you
have to let people earn that special spot in your life.
Stop giving it away girl. They laughed and laughed
until Lacy had to go and meet Keith for dinner.

They said their goodbyes and Maria sat back wondering what if Marcus is not the one? As Lacy was leaving Marcus pulled up,

Him and Maria ended up in a small disagreement because Maria had questioned him about his cell phone going off, he replied baby please don' t do this. It' s just a phone, I am here with you. Maria calmed down and agreed, she got into his car, and they went to grab something to eat.

On the way back Maria started asking Marcus what his intentions were for their future. Marcus said well, I would like to get married someday, maybe have a playmate for Eric and live happily ever after. Maria smiled and was glowing thinking about the same thing for the future.

Once back at the apartment Marcus and Maria ate cuddled and went to bed.

CHAPTER FIFTEEN

"The pressure is on"

Maria had started studying for her drivers license, she knew that would change her and Eric's life. Instead of depending on public transportation all the time, two months had gone pass and she had finally got her license. She was so happy.

Marcus seemed happy but was not because he knew Maria's next move was getting a car. And sure, enough it was, she bought her a little silver Chrysler for $1500.00 dollars. Now Maria and Eric were rolling.

She was getting home from work quicker, able to pick up Eric run errands, etc. Maria was smiling a whole lot more with being able to get around safer.

Marcus had pulled up to his house right after he got off work and boom Maria pulled up and parked next to him. Of course, Marcus acted happy to see her but knew he had to think of something fast because Kaye was about to come around in 20 minutes or so.

As Marcus got out of the car, he started saying here we go? Here we go. Maria said I'm not staying I was just in the neighborhood so I thought I would swing by. Trust me you can carry on.

Marcus was thinking in the back of his mind thank heaven. Maria kissed him on the lips and beeped the horn as she pulled away.

Meanwhile Marcus headed into the house to get ready for Kaye. He jumped into the shower with Maria on his mind, he was thinking about her pulling up the way that she did and was wondering that he may eventually get caught in one of his lies.

"Knock" "knock" The door broke his daze. It was Kaye, He jumped out of the shower and reached for his b-ball shorts and a towel, as he came down the stairs and opened the door Kaye was delighted at the view. She said umm, I know what to do with all that chocolate, Marcus replied well show me?

As they walked up the steps to the waterbed Kaye began to remove her top and threw it on the floor she started taking off her jeans and lace thongs, Marcus closed the door and began licking all over her breast and sucking them.

He put his fingers into her pussy to feel her getting wetter and wetter. As he came out of his shorts his dick was at a full erection, and he was ready.

Kaye laid him down on the waterbed and began to suck his thickness she rubbed his balls and sucked harder and harder, as she climbed up on top of him. She went back and forth harder and harder,

Marcus slowly placed his fingers in her ass as he grabbed her ass cheek with his other hand for her to ride him faster. As he pulled her deeper ,she began to moan louder and louder, Marcus quickly reached for her mouth because he wasn't sure if his mother was home.

Kaye giggled a little bit and then went back into motion. Marcus grabbed the remote and turned the TV up louder, Kaye began to moan as they both exhaled together.

Marcus kissed her and told her he had to leave in an hour, so she had a little time to relax before he dropped her around the corner.

Maria and Eric had just finished up with dinner when the cell phone rang, Eric looked down and saw that it was Marcus calling and asked his mom if he could answer it, she said it was ok.

As Eric said hello Marcus said hey sexy, Eric said I don' t think so. Marcus laughed and said ahh your right, hey there champ, Eric said hey Marcus are you coming over before my bedtime, he said yup I am on my way now.

Eric said I will have the game set up and he gave the phone to his mom, Marcus said hey sexy, Maria smiled and said what time should we expect you? He said very soon she said ok and they hung up the phone.

As Marcus pulled up, he had a small dessert in his hand for Maria and Eric. He used his key and Eric came running towards the steps he grabbed the dessert and began to open it up.

Maria said bet. It was a small chocolate cake, and they were both ready for that tasty treat. After they ate Marcus played the game with Eric until it was his bedtime an then him and Maria watched a little TV before they went to bed.

The next morning around 4:30 am Marcus heard glass break and hurried out to his car for work. Glass was all over the place all of his windows had been bashed out and he did not want Maria to know so he cleaned up some of it and called out of work as he drove home slowly to contact his insurance company.

As he pulled onto his block he began to wonder who would want to break out all of his windows at Maria's place? He started thinking is Maria seeing someone else.

As he called the insurance company to report vandalism on his vehicle, they asked him if he had any enemies who would want to do this to his car Marcus explained that he did not have any enemies and that he believes it was random, he had full coverage, so it was going to be covered after he paid his deductible.

The tow truck came and picked up his car and set him up for a loaner Marcus picked up his rental and went back to his house to think about a few things. Meanwhile Maria was wondering why she did not feel Marcus leave. She tried calling and he never answered. Normally he would at least kiss her forehead before leaving out to work.

She got her and Eric ready for the day and jumped in her car and left out of the apartment. After she dropped Eric off and got to work, she tried calling Marcus again, but he still did not answer.
She began to wonder if something was wrong.

By the time Maria got off work she refused to call Marcus anymore. She picked up Eric and grabbed dinner and went straight home, upon getting there she had a voicemail on her cell phone.

It was from Kaye leaving her a message saying that she needed to know who Maria was and she found her number in Marcus passenger side mirror in the visor. Sure, enough that is where Maria had placed her card.

CHAPTER SIXTEEN

"Facing the Truth"

Maria was very shocked that a female was on her line she was very hurt and had to ask where, do you know Marcus from! Kaye explained that she lived around the corner and that she had been seeing Marcus for several months.

Maria then said no sweetie Marcus and I have been together for two years and some change and he has been faithful to my knowledge I need more.

It is evident that you have been in his car, and I guess you have been getting fucked but that's probably it.

Kaye began to explain that she followed Marcus to Maria's apartment and bashed out all of his windows this morning, she said you can look in the back of your apartment and you will see the glass.

Maria quickly glanced out the window and saw all the broken glass from this morning. Then it dawned on her why Marcus had not called her yet.

Maria told Kaye she had to go but before she hung up Kaye told her that they would be going to AC next weekend, and she would know because he would say he was going with his boys. Maria said yeah ok and just hung up the phone.

Kaye called Marcus to then tell him what she had done. Back track to Maria's suspicion, every time she would leave out her apartment to go to the market or visit her mom Marcus would use the house phone to talk to his mother and a female, but Maria never knew who the female was because Marcus would just call her baby.

Maria had gotten a mini tape recorder from radio shack that linked into the line of her phone and would record the call each time her home phone was used. So, she already knew someone existed she just didn't know who, so to be able to put a name with the face was what she needed.

As she began to sit back and take a deep breath Marcus was coming thru the door, Eric ran to greet him Maria was upset but had to hold it in because she wasn't ready to discuss it with Marcus.

As Marcus went to kiss her, she pecked his lips as if nothing was wrong realizing that she had to suck this one up for a minute and hold out until next weekend, she knew she had Eric next weekend and it was a possibility that Kaye was telling the truth.

Kaye had told Marcus what happened but of course if Maria didn't bring it up then in Marcus mind, he wasn't really sure if Maria really knew. Maria carried on like nothing was wrong. So, Marcus did too.

She fed Marcus the leftovers as he played with Eric until his bedtime then Marcus and Maria talked small talk and went to bed.

The next morning Maria had five missed calls from Kaye, and Marcus phone was ringing off the hook too. Maria had her phone on silent because she figured the girl would call her when she couldn't reach Marcus.

Marcus got up jumped in the shower kissed Maria and left for work, Maria was unaware that Marcus had a rental, and Marcus did not let her know. When Maria got up, her and Eric got ready she had a hundred dollars and Eric had ten dollars they did their happy dance right on out the door.

Maria figured why mess up a good thing she has been in this relationship for over two years. She said she would call her best friend and take it from there.

When Maria got off work, she called Lacy and told her everything that was going on. Lacy said is he still giving you money, Maria said yes, helping with bills and all. Lacy said lay low and keep calm. She said he is not your husband and its fair game.

Maria was like I'm not going to allow him to disrespect me. Lacy said it's no longer about disrespect he already did that now it's about knowledge. He bought it to your door, only sloppy men do that shit, he has allowed this trick to follow him to your door. Game on.

Maria said bet telling her about the AC trip next weekend, Lacy said I have an idea, Maria quietly listened and took mental notes, agreeing with the plan and sticking too it,

No sex just talk, and money hit him where it hurts. Normally Maria was not into playing games, but her heart was in this over two and a half years. How dare this man be cheating on me, what did I do to deserve this?

All the guilt of the day was settling in on Maria, she was devastated. Yet she knew she had to pull it together. I'm a lot of things but I am nobody's fool.

CHAPTER SEVENTEEN

"The Weekend is here"

Thursday was finally here Marcus came over right after work and Maria was ready, she had brought dinner in with her and Eric kissed Marcus and made the plates, they had dessert and started playing games with Eric.

By this time Marcus had his car back so he didn't have to lie about where it was anymore, but Maria had already known, courtesy of Kaye, one thing for sure and two things for certain if you listen to a female enough, she will grant you the key to the next move. And sure, enough Maria had the next move.

As they finished up the game with Eric he went to bed, Maria began to ask Marcus about money to take Eric away for the weekend, she explained that the prior funds he gave her was used on the rent and the bills, she said she needed $600.00.

Marcus face looked stunned, but he agreed to give her the money the next morning. He also told her that he had to go away for his job from Friday night till Sunday, Maria happily smiled and said no problem baby, and I pray you have a safe trip.

The next morning Maria had the $600.00 dollars, and Marcus had gone to work, he even left an extra $20.00 for Eric to have. When they got up, they did a double happy dance as they got dress to begin their day.

Maria dropped Eric off and kept it moving to work. After work she called up Lacy to see what she was doing and told her she would swing by to pick her up for a few so they can execute the next steps in the plan.

Meanwhile in AC Kaye and Marcus were just checking into the Trump Towers Marcus asked Kaye to put the room on her credit card and he would give her the money back sometime next week.

At first, she went to question him but then she just pulled out her credit card and paid for the room. The cashier gave her the two room key cards and they proceeded to their room.

When they got inside Marcus explained to Kaye that he would have very little money for the weekend trip because his mother asked him for money towards some bills right before he left.

Kaye said it was fine because he always pays when they go out and he gives her money all the time. Marcus pecked her lips and said he would be right back, he returned within minutes with roses in his hand as he gave them to Kaye he said here for a beautiful lady, now get changed so we can go eat.

They walked about a mile up the boardwalk to a nice burger spot, holding hands until they were seated, Kaye ordered a double stacked burger with the works and Marcus followed suite with the same thing but with bacon and fries.

Kaye said I will eat a few of your fries, he ordered a coke, and she had an ice tea, they talked about starting a future as they waited for their food to come.

Kaye looked into Marcus eyes and said we should get a place together, Marcus said oh no too soon for that slow down it's coming. As the food came, they started eating and continued talking.

Marcus began to tell Kaye that he was falling in love with her, and he wanted to take things slow and make sure that he was making the right decision as they move forward.

Meanwhile back in Philly Maria and Lacy had stopped to grab a bite to eat at Tiffany's on the Blvd, one of Maria's favorite spots, she ordered some French toast and sausage along with an orange juice, and Lacy ordered some cream chipped beef with an apple juice, they loved breakfast no matter what time of day it was.

So, Maria what's up? He is in AC with another woman, now what? Well, I was thinking I knew this was coming and I am sure there are others. Maria chimed in why of course. Thank heaven I am not married going thru this, yet I have to now ask myself am I up for this challenge?

How long can I do this when Eric Is involved, He doesn't deserve this. Lacy said and neither do you. Do you think he even loves me? I mean how can someone do this cheat and run around with another woman like I don't exist?

Girl, you are talking to a victim, been there done that they laughed after they ate and continued to male bash men while thinking of Maria's next move.

Maria dropped Lacy off home, picked up Eric and headed home herself.

As she was opening her door Marcus was calling, she said hello and he said hey, baby how did your day go, Maria replied it's still going, I am just getting in, about to feed Eric and get settled, why don't you call me back in about an hour.

Marcus said baby you know I am away on business for my job I have a meeting in about fifteen minutes, Maria said Well, you better break away in an hour and call me. Talk to you then, as a matter of fact, make it two hours. She hung up quickly.

Marcus just stared at the phone and shook his head, Maria laughed so hard after hanging up she had to laugh to keep from crying.

Eric had finished his dinner and Maria told him to pack some fun clothes because they were going on a quick trip. Eric got excited asking where too, and Maria said go-kart racing in Hershey PA. Maria had booked the trip and decided she was going to have some fun on Marcus dime.

As her and Eric arrived at the Hershey Hotel, they were greeted by a great staff they had Hershey assorted candies from the lobby to the room, fresh fruit, chocolate milk, hoagies, and soda, this was a no rule weekend trip. No worries either.

Eric and Maria had so much fun but now it was time for bed. As they showered and jumped into their king sized, beds Eric said mom this bed is huge, it could fit me, you, Marcus and all of my cousins in it, Maria agreed as she turned on the TV and tuned into Eric's favorite cartoons.

Marcus had called back but Maria did not answer. Sweet Dreams Player she thought in her mind. Game on.

Kaye looked puzzled as to why Marcus kept stepping away as if he had something to hide, and he did, as he continued to try and call Maria, it was kind of ruining the nice weekend he thought he was going to have with Kaye but now he was more concerned with what Maria was up too.

Kaye tried to make a suggestion of walking on the beach when Marcus said maybe later, let's just go back to the room for a minute, get into some you and me time, we didn't come here to get wet on the beach when we can get wet in the room, Kaye smiled and followed him back to the room.

As they entered the room Kaye came out of her dress and Marcus was loving the bra and thong set that she had on, it gripped every curve perfectly, it was a light blue set with lace in all the right spots, he erected on sight.

He pulled down her bra strap and started sucking her breast and finger fucking her pussy, as she moaned, he knew she was ready, he pulled down his sweatpants and unveiled his thickness, as he progressed into her pussy she moaned louder and grabbed his shoulders tightly, she began to pull him closer and deeper into her wetness,

Marcus whispered in her ear I love this, and she said I love you. Kaye began to moan louder, and Marcus was trying not to cum but as Kaye started to keep more and more in rhythm with Marcus they both couldn't help it.

As they reached their climax Marcus released his juices all inside of her and she was in pure bliss. They rolled over and went to sleep for the night.

Back in Hershey, morning had come, and Maria and Eric were up and out, heading to the big go-kart racetrack in Hershey. Eric's smile on his face got bigger and bigger the closer they got to the track, it reminded him of the super Mario track from his game he always played.

Maria pulled out their wrist bands that she had previously paid for, they had unlimited time on the track, she was just praying that her little man could keep up.

Keep up is what he did, once he jumped in the blue go-kart, he was out Maria jumped into the green one, and tried to catch up to him.

They laughed and raced around the track for a few hours. Eric was so excited to be actually driving by himself. Maria was happy she hadn't had this much fun in a long time.

After the race which Eric won of course, it was time to eat, Eric wanted chicken fingers and fries, and Maria ate a grilled chicken salad. They shared a coke and headed back to the hotel.

Maria looked at her phone and realized Marcus had called her eight times. She thought to herself I will call him when we get settled.

After her and Eric ate their Hershey treats, she let him watch cartoons while she returned Marcus call. He picked up the call immediately. Hey baby how is your day going? Maria replied it is going fine, Eric and I are in Hershey Pa enjoying this beautiful day.

Marcus said oh really, a 600-hundred-dollar beautiful day, yes of course said Maria, we are going horseback riding and walking thru the Hershey factory before we leave tomorrow. We are having so much fun, how is your business trip going?

Oh, it's moving along Marcus said, not as much fun as you guys are having, thou, wish I was there. Maria laughed and said I wish you were here too but maybe another time player, Marcus said why do you keep saying player to me?

Do you not believe that I am where I am telling you? Maria said oh yes, I believe you are in AC. Marcus said yes on a business trip, yes a business trip Maria giggled, and well ok I guess you should get back to that.

Call me to say good night. Marcus said will do and then hung up. Eric asked Maria was that Marcus and she said yes you can talk to him when he calls to say good night.

A few hours went by, and sure enough Marcus was on the line, Eric answered the phone and began talking to Marcus, telling him about Hershey and the go-karts, Marcus said it will be a better trip next time because he will be there.

Maria took the phone after Eric said goodnight. She spoke with Marcus and said see you tomorrow when you get back from your trip.

The next morning Maria and Eric went horseback riding and then walked thru the Hershey factory before hitting Hershey Park to get on lots of rides in the amusement park before heading home.

They loaded up the car and left. The drive home was nice and relaxing. Maria was so happy to arrive home. She and Eric unpacked kicked off their shoes and relaxed.

It was Sunday in A.C. and Kaye was really bothered that things had not really gone her way in the midst of being away with Marcus for the weekend.

It was almost like his mind was somewhere else, more like on someone else, and sure enough it was, Maria was on his mind heavy, her little surprise trip had Marcus mind spinning.

As he arrived back in Philly, he dropped Kaye off home and headed straight for Maria's place. As he entered it was quiet, he looked and saw that they were both sleeping tired after their trip from Hershey, he kissed Maria and told her he would be back later, she nodded her head ok.

CHAPTER EIGHTEEN

"Hurting all over"

Marcus headed to meet up with Maurice and Kevin, they were meeting to talk about some comedy skits and putting together something to start doing shows, when they started messing around with the basketball in the playground out west.

As Marcus reached for the ball he twisted and broke his ankle. Maurice called the ambulance and Marcus was taken to the hospital. After he was seen he had a cast placed on his left ankle and he was going to be out of work for a few weeks.

He called Maria to let her know what had happened, she was worried, he told her that Maurice was taking him home, she said ok get some rest and call me tomorrow.

Marcus called Kaye and explained what had happened she said she would be right around when Marcus gets home. As he arrived Kaye was there to help bring him into the house, as her and Maurice got him up the steps and into his room, he began to feel the pain kicking in.

Kaye gave him more meds and tucked him in she stayed with him thru the night incase he needed anything.

The next morning Kaye had to go to work she gave Marcus more meds and then left. Ten minutes later Maria pulled up she had dropped Eric at school and came straight to see about Marcus.

Marcus little brother was outside and let Maria into the house. As Maria started up the stairs, she heard Marcus trying to make it to the bathroom, she quickly grabbed his crutches because he almost fell.

Perfect timing baby, Maria said yeah you think. Let me help you. He used the restroom and she helped him back into his room. She said are you hungry he said yes, she said I will order us something and pick it up around at the store.

As they ate and talked Marcus explained what had happened telling Maria he twisted his ankle and broke it. She said you have to be more careful baby.

He said I have a doctors appt on Tuesday and Thursday.

Maria said I can take you on Thursday. He said ok he would see if his brother could take him to the Tuesday appt.

Marcus was in so much pain but wanted Maria to ride him. She laughed at him and said boy you must be crazy; I'm not trying to hit my leg on that cast. He said but baby I'm hurting so bad feeling your pussy will make me feel so much better.

Maria said boy please here take some more meds. She got his clothes out for the appt tomorrow and told him she would see him later in the week to take him to his Thursday appt.

Tuesday came and Kaye was over to take Marcus to his first appt. as they arrived at The University of Penn Marcus got into a wheelchair and Kaye pushed him to the unit to sign in.

As she signed him in the receptionist said ID and insurance card for him, please pretty lady, Kaye reached into Marcus wallet and got it out. The receptionist then said please be seated and wait to be called.

Marcus Hall, Kaye said coming, as she wheeled Marcus to the back to see the doctor.
When they came out the receptionist said we will see you on Thursday, Marcus said will do. And Kaye said goodbye.

Kaye got Marcus into the car and back home to rest she ordered them something to eat sat with him for awhile and then left.

Rose had been calling Marcus phone because he had not been to see her at the Picka Dilly. Marcus answered his phone and told her what had happen she said I'm so sorry to hear this. She then paused and said she had something to tell Marcus.

He said what is it? She said I'm pregnant and I only slept with you. Marcus told her that he was in a lot of pain, and he would be down for a few weeks but if she could make an appointment for an abortion, he would pay for it. She agreed and said hope you feel better.

It was now the middle of the week and Maria had paid a sitter for Eric and they were taking him to school on Thursday, she grabbed some food and arrived over Marcus house to spend the night and take him to his appointment in the morning.

He was still in so much pain, she fed him and gave him his meds and let him nod back off to sleep.

She jumped in the shower and then laid in bed next to him. His phone kept going off, but Maria already knew, so she just went to sleep.

The morning came and Maria helped Marcus get ready and she got dressed, they were ready to go. As they arrived down at the University of Penn Maria grabbed a wheelchair and started pushing Marcus towards his doctors' office, as they arrived, she approached the receptionist desk and signed him in.

The receptionist said oh Marcus so glad to see you again you must enjoy having lovely women pushing you around. Maria took kind to the compliment and said thank you, but it also didn't go over her head. She thought about the compliment "Lovely women" yeah ok.

As the doctor called Marcus to the back Maria quickly pushed him to the back. Marcus was seen and then they were out. As they drove to Maria's place, she asked him what did the receptionist mean by lovely Women pushing him around?

He laughed it off and said where are we getting something to eat from? I think I want Taco Bell. Maria said yeah ok. As she pulled into the Taco Bell drive thru right off of 5th & Luzerne. They ordered a box of soft tacos knowing that Eric was going to enjoy the food.

Marcus was still in a lot of pain and hadn't thought about going up the stairs at Maria's place. Maria turned into a park at Eric's school he came running out, he was excited to see Marcus and even more excited to see the box from Taco Bell. He jumped in the back seat and said let's get home fast I'm hungry Marcus said yeah me and you both.

Maria parked the car and gave the tacos to Eric to carry up she said don't drop them. She then helped Marcus out of the car and gave him his crutches, he said darn baby the stairs she said well it's not like you have to go anywhere once you are up there.

It took Marcus ten minutes to get up the steps, Eric had washed his hands and was waiting to eat some tacos, Maria started setting the table, and Marcus was tired after finally getting to the top step.

Maria was laughing inside because she knew he was in pain. They sat down to eat, and Marcus took his meds and started talking to Maria.

They ate off paper plates, so Eric started cleaning up and wiping off the table Maria was listening as Marcus started telling her about his ankle and the possibility of a case and suing the city because he had broken his ankle on a city playground.

He was saying that Maria should have known that he could sue. Maria said I had no idea you could sue for twisting and breaking your own ankle,

Kaye had told Marcus about suing the city, Marcus, friend Keith had gone back up to the playground and hammered the spot that Marcus had fell. Back then city playgrounds had no cameras.

Of course, it would take a few months for the city to settle, Marcus had a good attorney and knowing what the case was worth the attorney was moving quickly to settle so that he could get his cut.

A few months had passed, and Marcus was finally out of his cast and back into his old shoes (if you know what I mean). He started back working and getting back into his comedy skits.

He was preparing to do little appearances at Champagnes on Chelten Ave, along with little spots out West Philly. He was starting to make people laugh. Maria was seeing little flyers around down her end in Logan about his little late -night shows, she was truly unbothered.

Marcus would still come over and use his key, but Maria was too busy getting her studies on to become a community health educator at Thomas Jefferson University. She had her and Eric's future to think about.

CHAPTER NINTEEN

"Petals and Tears"

Marcus phone rang and it was Rose, it had been a few months since she called while waiting for Marcus to come handle his business. She was now 12 weeks pregnant and starting to show, she was still in school and still working at the Dilly.

Marcus said Rose how are you, she said I am fine, but I was wondering if you were still going to take care of this for me, my money is tight and I'm running out of time.

Marcus said make the appointment and I will meet up with you and give you the money, she explained that he would have to go with her, and she had no idea where to go and have it done. Marcus told her he knew a place and not to worry.

Meet me Thursday at Broad and Olney, there is a little place on Tabor Rd. that does the procedure actually I will make the appointment for Wednesday because there is a 24- hour waiting period, and you can have it done on Thursday. Rose agreed to meet him there on Wednesday.

Marcus headed down to Maria's place he stopped and picked up dinner and dessert, as he entered the apartment, he heard Maria talking on the phone, so he waited at the bottom of the stairs for a minute.

Maria was talking to Lacy saying how discouraged she feels and believes Marcus isn't being faithful. Marcus slammed the downstairs door and Maria told Lacy she had to go.

Eric ran to the steps and was happy to see Marcus, he smiled grabbed the dessert and put it on the table. Maria took the dinner from him and placed it on the table to, not knowing if Marcus had heard her on the phone.

He washed his hands and grabbed the plates and began making them, Eric was the only one not quiet. He began to tell Marcus about his day and how he left his skate- board, at his school and he hopes nobody takes it. Maria chimed in and said it will be there in the morning trust me.

Marcus said Eric I will drop you at school in the morning Maria's eyes lifted and was shocked, Marcus said he had an appointment up this end and could take Eric to school. Ok Maria said. As they finished up dinner Eric ran to turn on the game so he could play Marcus before bedtime.

Maria cleaned the kitchen and jumped in the shower and then the bed. Marcus soon followed.

Morning came and Marcus and Eric left out while Maria was getting ready for work, she noticed Marcus still left her a hundred dollars and she did her little dance out the door.

Marcus dropped Eric at school and told him he would be picking him up, and not to forget his skate- board that he took in yesterday for show and tell. Eric said ok and hopped out and ran in the building.

Marcus then went to Tabor Road to set up the appointment for Rose the next day. As he entered the building, he was hoping he could make the appointment for Rose.

He walked into the receptionist area and signed in, he was called next, and he said I need to make an appointment for my girlfriend to terminate a pregnancy.

The receptionist handed him some paperwork to fill out and said have her bring this back in the morning when you return. Marcus said okay took the paperwork and left.

Marcus called Rose an explained that he would be dropping the paperwork to her this afternoon and could she fill it out and be ready to meet him at Broad and Olney in the morning.

Rose began to ask Marcus more personal questions, one being do you have any children? Marcus said none of my own. My lady has a son. Rose asked! Well, are you sure you want me to do this? Marcus said I don't even know you Rose. This is not how I would want to start a family.

Rose said she understood, and that she would see him when he came by. Marcus hung up feeling empty, he was very agitated and hurt by her words, and how could you want to keep a baby with a man you don't even know? He shook his head and continued back up the way to West Philly.

As he pulled into a parking spot in front of his door, he got out grabbed the mail and began to open it, there was a letter from his attorney saying that the city had settled for 450,000.00 he would receive 325,000.00 of that. Marcus was so excited,

He ran in the house and up the stairs to share the news with his mother, she was happy. She started telling him what she needed done around the house and how she could use some of that money he said mom you know I got you.

Marcus changed his clothes and headed over to Rose spot to give her the paperwork for the appointment tomorrow. He was keeping his money under wraps he didn't want her to change her mind based on his financial come up

He called her phone as he pulled up her block, she answered, and he asked her to come outside and get the papers. As she opened the car door she sat inside and began to tell Marcus that she doesn't know if she can do it, he said listen I'm not taking care of no kid right now, if you have it, you will be on your own.

Rose explained that she herself was raised in foster care and wanted nothing more than a family. Marcus said yeah family we would not be one because I don't know you. And for that reason, you should fill out this paperwork and meet me in the morning. Rose said okay as a tear rolled down her face, Marcus was unbothered by the tears.

Marcus left Rose and raced back up to Olney to pick up Eric from school, Eric jumped in the car and said what's to eat? Marcus smiled and said hey little buddy lets grab something on our way in. What do you want? Eric said McDonalds, I don't think your mom will agree with that one Marcus said, Eric said awe man come on.

Marcus pulled into McDonald's right off of Tabor Rd and Adams and ordered a big happy meal two big macs and two fish filets with two large fries no drinks. Eric was so happy because his mom rarely fed him fast food, so he knew he was getting over on Marcus.

Marcus pulled out of McDonalds and went straight to the store to buy Maria some flowers to brighten up her night. As they pulled up and parked at the apartment Maria was just getting home. She said what's this? Eric said food and flowers just for you.

They went in and sat down to eat and after that relaxed and watched TV, Maria said oh staying another night are we, and nodded her head at Marcus. He said yes why you want me to leave, she said no it's fine.

The next morning Marcus dropped Eric at school, and he continued to meet Rose at Broad and Olney, she came to the car, and they drove around the corner to the clinic.

Once inside Rose gave the Receptionist her paperwork and sat down and waited to be called, when they called her name Marcus got up and paid for the procedure.

The nurse took Rose to the back they explained that if she was sure about having the procedure, she could do it today because someone had cancelled.

Rose said that she was sure no need for the 24 - hour waiting period if she could get it done today that would be fine. She had the exam and then the procedure.

Marcus was nervous because she was taking so long, when she came from the back, she told Marcus she needed to fill her prescription he said the pharmacy was right outside the building. He said they, did it? She said yes someone cancelled so I was able to get it done and over with.

As they exited the building to go into the pharmacy, Lacy was coming out. She said hey Marcus, he was shocked as he held the door Lacy looked at rose and said hi and kept going. Lacy did see that they came from the clinic next door.

Marcus saw her reach for her phone, and he already knew she was calling Maria. He continued in with Rose got the prescription filled and rushed to take Rose home and got her settled in. Marcus raced back down to Maria's place she wasn't there.

He then tried calling her cell phone she picked up and said she was in class right now and couldn't talk, she would call him back. Marcus just sat down in the apartment thinking about what he was going to say.

While he waited to grab Eric from school, he used the home phone to call Keith and Maurice and yes Maria still had the recorder hooked up to the phone line.

Marcus started telling them about Rose and seeing Lacy at the pharmacy and knowing that lacy was going to tell Maria about the situation, but he was going to tell Maria that it was his cousin and he had to pick her up from the clinic because his mom asked him too.

Maria came through the door, she had picked Eric up early from school, picked up dinner and came home. Lacy had called her and told her what happened but said let Marcus tell you that he saw me. Maria agreed to play along.

Marcus jumped up and started helping Maria set the table, he said a little early for dinner isn't it. She said no not if your hungry, Eric are you hungry? He said yes mom. She said come eat.

As they sat down Marcus began saying how he saw Lacy today while he was at the pharmacy with his cousin Rose, Maria said oh you have a cousin that lives up this way? He said no she went to the clinic up this way, Maria said oh! really?

Marcus said yes let's not talk about that so what are we doing this weekend? Think we can go go – kart racing? Eric yelled yes let's do it. Maria said sure why not. Marcus said we will go over to New Jersey this time.

CHAPTER TWENTY

"Here comes the money"

Marcus still hadn't told Maria about his settlement with the city or how much money he would be getting, He just wanted to wait and play, things by ear. He headed home to be able to think and clear his head.

As he pulled up and parked Kaye was pulling up behind him, He looked shocked she jumped out of her car and said what shocked to see me? He said a little. Kaye began to ask him about the settlement because she knew the attorney that she had referred him too.

They went inside and Marcus said he really didn't want to discuss it tonight. Kaye said okay and began to get undressed, she said let me help you take your mind off of all of this, she had on a red lace and silk bra and thong set, with some edible wraps for his dick, she wrapped one around his thick dick and started sucking the chocolate off of him.

Marcus was well erected and ready for this venture after all it had been along day. After Kaye licked and sucked the wrap off Marcus began to feel her breast and stuck his fingers into her mouth, he took his other hand and started finger fucking her, pushing his fingers in and out of her pussy, she was wet and he was ready.

He laid her down on the waterbed and began fucking her so hard he grabbed her neck sucked her breast hard and plunged in and out of her harder and harder she began to cry, he then turned her over and licked the back of her neck as he glided down towards her lower back, he turned her around and began licking her pussy and twirling his tongue all around inside of her.

He got up and forced his thickness into her and pushed back and forth until he released his pleasure all inside of her. She was tired she had never seen this side of him. She felt embarrassed as that wasn't making love, she felt like she had just been fucked. Marcus rolled over and went to sleep no hugs kiss or caress.

The next morning Kaye gathered her things and left. Marcus woke up and started taking care of business he went downtown to the attorney's office and signed the release for his money.

The first thing he did was purchase a duplex in Cobb's Creek around the corner from Kaye's mom's house. It was a great deal, and he would get to profit from it being as though he was still living with his mom.

He put two tenants into the duplex right away. He bought a new car, and he handed his mom a few thousand dollars while helping her fix up her house. At this point Maria wasn't visiting as much as she used to and Kaye was there a lot more.

The weekend came and Marcus pulled up to Maria's in his new car, Eric was excited to be going go-kart racing across the bridge, Maria played it sweet and promised herself that even though she heard the recording of Marcus about Rose this just wasn't the time.

As they arrived over in Jersey to the Go-Kart spot Eric jumped out and was amazed at all the colorful carts, they had yellow, blue, red, green, white, and black, way more colors than Hershey. He ran and jumped into the blue one because that was his favorite color. Maria took the yellow one, and Marcus took the black one.

As Maria pulled off to race her cell phone vibrated, it was Kaye, Maria, shook her head and let it go to voicemail. Marcus phone started to vibrate he couldn't answer it because he was racing Eric and Maria. As they raced each other around the track for the rest of the day they all had a ball.

Kaye was furious because she knew that Marcus had to be out with Maria because he wasn't answering his phone. She decided to leave Maria a voicemail telling her that she remembered where she lived and would be touching base with her one day this week.

Kaye knew Marcus got that money and was probably out spending some of it on Maria, the thought of it was making here more and more angry.

After go-kart racing Maria, Marcus and Eric grabbed a bite to eat at The Pub Restaurant, they ordered the biggest steaks and had all the toppings mushrooms, onions, green peppers, and steak sauce, with a side of loaded baked potatoes, and salad from the salad bar. Delicious Eric belted out this is a great place. Maria and Marcus nodded and agreed.

On the way home they were stuffed. To stuffed, for either of them to deal with the nasty voicemails that each of them received from Kaye. Marcus and Maria said nothing to each other about the voicemails. When they got in everybody was so tired, they went straight to bed.

The next morning Marcus had to work so he left out after kissing Maria, he left her $100 and Eric $20 they woke up and did their little happy dance to Mike's diner by Front and Godfrey, Eric ordered pancakes and Maria had her the basic bacon eggs over easy with cheese grits and toast with butter and jelly, and they both had a big glass of orange juice.

Marcus was at work but also studying for an up-coming comedy show that he had in Atlantic City, he was excited and looking forward to it. He couldn't tell Maria about the show because he was going with Kaye. He made sure not to post any flyers in Logan, Maria barely went out of the neighborhood and Marcus was banking on that.

Marcus phone rang and it was Kaye, asking where he was last night? Marcus said baby I was studying, and I really didn't have time for games I'm trying to make something of myself with this comedy. She said I understand but you could have at least answered my call.

Marcus said baby don't you worry your pretty little head we are going to make it big. Kaye smiled and said okay. He said after this show in AC it should put me on the map.

Marcus had more money, so you know that meant more women, He hung with Kaye, left work and went to meet up with a new friend name Lisa who lived in Germantown right off of Wayne. He met her when he did a show at Champagnes Lounge.

As he pulled up to Lisa's house, he was a little hesitant at a guy coming out of her place, he waited as the guy left and then he got out and knocked on the door. Lisa answered, she had on some booty shorts and a bra, Marcus asked her if she would like to go out? she said nah, my place is good we can watch a movie or something.

Marcus said cool I prefer chilling and hanging in, as he laughed heading to her bathroom. He looked into his wallet to make sure he had a condom because he really didn't like being without one with a new situation. He had one so he proceeded to Lisa's room where she was.

As he entered, she was out of her shorts and stretched across the bed. Marcus was thinking this is too easy I really better use this condom. He sat next to her, and she began to rub his dick, she said I always like to play with what I'm working with.

Marcus said well let me help you out, he pulled down his sweat pants and let her pull out his dick and play with it, she started stroking it and then licking it gently,

She then slid on top of it, he was amazed he didn't pull out the condom yet, as she started gliding back and forth across his dick, she was getting wetter and wetter and Marcus dick was getting harder and harder, he was thinking because it's new pussy he wanted to feel it first without the condom if she didn't say anything.

Sure, enough she said nothing, and her pussy hit the tip of his dick and his dick went in. Marcus moaned this pussy is so tight, Lisa said yes baby give it to me harder, Marcus grabbed her ass and began pulling her closer and deeper as he pushed deeper inside of her, he was enjoying the tightness of her pussy.

Lisa was holding on to his shoulders as she pulled him closer in her, he said are you on birth control, she said not yet but I will get on if you want me too. Marcus gave one deeper plunge into her pussy and then he pulled out right quick and ejaculated all over her stomach.

Lisa said damn, I was just about to explode all over you. Marcus said hold that thought as he reached for the condom, he put it on and went back inside of her, he felt that same tightness and he just couldn't control himself and released his cum into the condom. Lisa had released her juices all over herself she was satisfied and hoping that this wasn't her last time seeing Marcus.

As they washed off and got dressed Lisa said she was hungry. Marcus said what's around here, She said Champagnes. He said okay let's go. They arrived there and had the turkey crab burgers and Lisa had a drink. Marcus had a coke with his meal. After feeding her he dropped her home and headed to Maria's place.

He used his key to get in and Maria and Eric were just settling down, Eric jumped up and hugged Marcus, Maria was getting worried because of Eric's attachment to Marcus. As a mother she doesn't want Eric or herself, hurt by Marcus's selfishness.

After all she thought if there is a Kaye? I know there are more.

Marcus said you know I love you right, Maria
said sure, he said sure, your, not saying you love me
back, she said I do I'm just a little skeptical
sometimes. Your actions say otherwise, and I just
hope you are being faithful Marcus. He looked in
her eyes and said yes, I am Maria.

He said I'm trying out this comedy thing and
after that, things are going to get better for us. I
promise. Maria said okay if you say so.

Meanwhile Maria had a plan of her own in the
back of her mind because she already knew about
Kaye and she was sure there were others.

Marcus told her that he would not be staying the
night because he had to study his skits for a show he
had coming up. Maria said fine with me, and kissed
him, as he left, he handed her $400 dollars and said
I do love you. Maria said Money doesn't count
Marcus, it helps but money isn't love.

CHAPTER TWENTY -ONE

"Catch up to the game"

Marcus pulled up to his house while Kaye was parking her car right behind him. She got out and asked him what was up? He said what do you mean? She said you know what I mean. I know where you are coming from. Marcus said girl please, why don't you go to the gym or something you be thinking of crazy things.

Kaye said yeah okay you know I live right around the corner, Marcus said yeah, I know. As he went to his door Kaye went in with him and said she was spinning the night Marcus said okay. If I was seeing other women, would I keep allowing you to show up at my door and spend the night? She said I suppose not.

Marcus jumped into the tub to finish washing the scent of Lisa off of his body, and Kaye was in his room looking thru his things while getting undressed, as he came out of the bathroom, she quickly hid a phone number out of his phone that she wrote down.

They stretched across the bed and talked for a minute as Marcus turned to the porn channel and began to play with Kaye's breast.

She in turn started to play with herself placing her fingers inside of her and rubbing them across her clit. Marcus became aroused he turned her around and started rubbing her ass and putting his fingers into her pussy and then her ass and back to her pussy, she began to get wet in both areas.

He slipped his thickness into her pussy and began pushing in and out thrusting harder and harder as she moaned with pleasure it was surely a different version than last time when he made her cry. They both released their juices and went to bed.

In the morning Marcus jumped up and said let's go to breakfast, they drove to the South Street Diner and had steak and eggs, Kaye did not eat pork, on occasion Marcus would forget that. After breakfast Marcus dropped Kaye at home and went back home to study his skits for his show in AC.

Kaye drove to meet a new friend she had met named Damon; He was tall dark and handsome and actually looked a lot like Marcus they had a lot in common. Damon was in the military he was stationed down Virginia Beach but was here on an assignment.

As Kaye pulled up to Damon's place, she was a little hesitant because she didn't want to cheat on Marcus but also realized that he was seeing Maria and Rose she got her number out of Marcus cell phone. She had called Rose and found out about the abortion and the nights out at Dillies. Rose also told her about Maria. Even thou she already knew.

Damon came down to the door, He had his shirt off and his muscles were tight. Kaye was excited to be in his company tonight. Damon greeted her with a soft kiss and said I'm glad you could make it over. Kaye said yeah me too.

He had the music on playing some smooth jazz. Candles lit and some food on the table, the atmosphere was nice. Kaye sat down on the couch and Damon poured her and him a glass of merlot. As they started sipping, he asked her if she was hungry and then grabbed the shrimp and salmon bites from the table for her to nibble on.

After about an hour they were both tipsy and horny, Kaye started to undress Damon with her eyes, and he already had her undressed in his mind. He held her hand and then guided her to his bedroom he had nice soft think mattresses Kaye noticed.

He began to get undressed he grabbed Kaye and started playing with her short hair running his fingers thru it she was getting hotter, and wetter. Damon started taking off her shirt, and he enjoyed the lace bra that she was wearing. He pulled down her bra strap and admired her perky breast.

He began sucking her nipples and stroking her neck, she began to take off her pants and panties, as he took her hand and placed it on his thickness.

She started rubbing it harder and harder he placed his fingers into her mouth, and she started licking his fingers he got harder and asked her was she ready. She replied yes,

He laid her down on her back and lifted her legs over his shoulders as he thrust his thickness inside of her, she moaned and moved a little because he was bigger than Marcus, and she had to adjust her flow to match his.

She began to pull him deeper inside of her, he was pushing softly but hard enough to feel her grip his dick. They were both enjoying each others pleasure with no condom, Kaye said to Damon let me ride you, they switched position. Kaye was now on top thrusting back and forth as Damon grabbed her in deeper to him, they both exploded in pleasure.

He held her through the night and into the morning, as he told her he would only be here for one more week. Kaye said as long as you keep in touch I don't care where you go. He made her breakfast and then she went home.

Kaye got home and jumped into the shower. She was ashamed of cheating but felt well justified. She was off from work today and hadn't told anyone she just cuddled up and relaxed the whole day by herself. She called Damon to let him know that she really enjoyed herself and hoped they could do it again soon.

CHAPTER TWENTY -TWO

"The Beginning to the end"

About a month had gone by and Maria was getting tired of Marcus sudden disappearances and him blaming it on the comedy skits and practices after all he never really invited her to many shows saying the shows were late at night, and she had Eric.

Their sex life was a little different because Maria was scared that if he was in the streets, she didn't want to catch whatever he was out there getting.

Maria was home chilling and Kaye called her phone, Maria answered and said hello, the voice said hey it's me Kaye, I was wondering if you were still seeing Marcus, of course I am and stop calling my dam phone. Kaye said whatever and hung up.

By this time Maria was furious and Marcus was pulling up, she waited for him to come inside, and then boom the question just came flooding out. Who the fuck is Kaye and why is she calling my phone? Marcus was shocked and didn't know what to say.

Baby that's my cousin, no Marcus she is not your cousin. Ding, want to try again? Baby seriously she is my cousin. Marcus she is not your cousin she called my phone and told me that you are seeing her you took her to AC, and on some other little trips. I'm waiting?

Marcus slammed his hand on Maria's glass table and broke it glass shattered everywhere. Marcus looked up and ran into the bathroom. Maria tried to open the bathroom door.

She decided oh you want to break glass, she grabbed her gulf clubs and ran down the stairs and outside to Marcus new Gold Maxima She Slammed the gulf club down on the front windshield and glass shattered all over the place, she then did the back glass and all the windows in between.

As she did that the police were pulling up because Marcus had called them from in the bathroom. When they got out the car he came down.

He went to one officer while Maria was talking to the other. They didn't arrest anyone because when they went upstairs to the apartment, they saw Maria's apartment was riddled with glass from her broken tables by Marcus.

They just took a report and left. Marcus pulled off in his car with all his broken windows while shaking his head, Maria went into her apartment and started cleaning up before Eric got home from school.

She threw out the entire dinette set, and a TV that had fell over and broke. She was so disappointed in Marcus. The lies had become the true fabric of who he was, and Maria was very upset.

Marcus kept calling her, but Maria wouldn't answer. He wanted to explain his self, but Maria just didn't want to hear anymore lies.

She called her mother and her best friend Lacy to tell them what had happened. She explained Kaye calling her home and then Marcus coming over and breaking the table and her breaking the glass out of his car windows, Maria was not proud at all for being placed in this situation.

The next day Marcus was at Maria's door saying how sorry he was and what could he do to make it up to her? Maria said you can start by buying a new TV and dinette set for the kitchen. He went and bought a TV and had the dinette set delivered the same day.

Maria said thank you and have a nice day. Marcus was like wait a minute let me talk to you. Maria said you are a liar and a cheater there is nothing to say. He said let me explain. Maria said you have two minutes.

He began to tell Maria that Kaye was a friend, and she was crazy because he slept with her once and she just became obsessed. Started stalking him and whomever he was seeing.

Maria calmed down and let Marcus come inside the apartment. She began to tell him about the recorder and the things that she knew, Kaye, Rose having an abortion and she asked Marcus why? He said he was sorry she said sorry isn't good enough.

Maria started crying and asked Marcus if he could leave because she didn't want a repeat of yesterday. He jumped in his rental and pulled off. Maria sat at her new table and cried, All the money in the world couldn't replace that ache in her heart.

Kaye kept calling Maria's phone, Maria answered what the hell do you want? Kaye said I know he told you I was crazy, Maria said yes and to keep calling my phone I believe that you are.

Kaye started telling Maria about the duplex and the tenants and that she thought Marcus was dating a tenant in the duplex. Maria said she didn't care. Kaye said well what about the comedy show he has coming up in AC? Maria again responded I don't care. Kaye said well what about Rose? Maria said what about her? I don't care.

Kaye said what do you care about? Maria said my life my son, my soul. And she hung up. Kaye kept trying to call her back, but Maria would not answer, she also did not answer Marcus.

Maria just sat back and wondered what her next move would be. Maria called out of work and just paced back and forth for most of the day, unaware that her voicemail was now full, from Lacy, Kaye and Marcus. Maria was just trying to block out everyone to keep from having a nervous breakdown.

Maria finally returned Kaye's call and then Kaye explained how they all could find out the truth, and the truth was all Maria wanted. Finally, the plan was set. Maria called Marcus and asked him to come over, he said he would be there around 6 she said perfect. As she awaited his arrival, she had a few questions she needed answered herself.

Eric had got in from school and Maria had told him to do his homework in her room and not to come out unless she called for him no matter what he heard going on. There was one exception she said I need you to lock the bolt lock when Marcus arrives and take the extra key into the room with you.

Eric agreed Maria quickly made him a snack and had another one waiting in her room for him because he might be there for awhile. She told him to go to the bathroom now, and not to make any noise once he did what he was told.

Maria put her first surprise in the bathroom and as the second surprise arrived, she put her in the living room closet. Everything was ready to go. As she sat back and waited for 6:00 to come. It was 5:45pm and it was the longest fifteen minutes ever, but it was finally here.

Marcus came in using his key, Eric said hello and ran downstairs and locked the bolt lock. He came back up and hugged Marcus and ran into his mothers, room turned the TV up loud and closed the door.

Marcus got relaxed in the living room, took off his sneakers and got comfy. Maria came out the kitchen with a quick snack for him and started talking. Hey baby I really need to talk with you about this girl Kaye that keeps calling my phone.

Marcus said baby I told you that girl is crazy she has mental issues. She keeps coming to my house and threatening me, seriously Maria, I only love you. Before he could even get another lie out of his mouth Kaye came busting out of the closet.

Marcus mouth dropped open and he started putting on his shoes, Kaye said now, what is this shit that you are talking saying that I'm crazy? She stepped up in Marcus face waiting for his response. He said wait a minute you are crazy and stalking me, why are you here? Maria chimed in to get to the bottom of this.

Kaye said you told me you weren't seeing Maria. Marcus said well I'm not we are friends. Maria said excuse me friends. Marcus said well lately. Maria said what about the key you just used to get in. Marcus said but I don't live here.

Maria started shaking her head. She plugged in the iron and was letting it heat up because she knew he couldn't get out of the apartment without the key.

She couldn't believe she had stooped this low, but hey we are all here now and the truth is about to come out.

Kaye was still yelling and trying to get answers out of Marcus. She said are you going to tell us the truth or what. Maria came in the living room with the hot iron and threw it at Marcus she said I want the truth now. Marcus blocked the iron but burnt his hand while doing it.

Kaye said tell her. I was with you when you broke your ankle got your money bought a duplex around the corner from my mom's house. Tell her. Marcus said yes this is true. Maria had tears rolling down her face she didn't know what to say.

All of a sudden, she opened up the bathroom door and said Rose can you come out and clarify any other doubts that may be in my mind. Marcus was shocked to see Rose he yelled what the fuck is going on why is she here.

Rose said I am here because I had an abortion by you. You came to the Dilly at least twice a week to fucking see me and fuck me. I got pregnant and you took me to Tabor Rd to have an abortion. Maria said that was you? Rose said yes. This was right after he broke his ankle.

Maria began to cry I can't believe you did this to me. She started swinging on him beating him up with her gulf club, Kaye and Rose jumped in and they all started beating his ass. He couldn't get away.

Kaye finally screamed stop because I'm pregnant, and I won't be having an abortion.

Marcus looked up at her, and Maria was in shock. Rose said I was only fucking him for the money can you let me out now please. Maria grabbed the key and went down and unlocked the door. Rose left,

Kaye was upstairs crying and screaming I'm pregnant I'm pregnant. Marcus ran out of the apartment and left. Maria watched as Kaye came down and left too.

Maria was speechless even though she had recorded conversations of Marcus she never really listened to all of them. and figured now was the time.

She pulled out all of the recordings and listened to how unfaithful Marcus had really been his conversations with Maurice and Keith had revealed nothing but sex, money and lies.

Even Marcus's mother knew he was seeing Kaye and Maria, what a bitch Maria thought. I know that's your son, but you are a woman first. Damn.

Maria was so hurt after listening to everything, her whole life with this man was a lie. He was a lie. Marcus Hall was a cheater a user a liar.

CHAPTER TWENTY -THREE

"Back to Reality"

Maria thought back to the beginning of her and Marcus relationship when she went over his mother's house and his mom lied about the flowers and the vase. She shook her head and said I should have left him alone then.

Marcus kept trying to call Maria and she wouldn't answer, He would stop by her mothers and leave five hundred dollars every two weeks for months for Maria and Eric.

Kaye ended up having a baby boy she named him after Marcus. That would be his only child. He was proud of the fact that he finally had a child that was claimed by him.

Maria tried to move on with her life by putting the pieces back together for her and Eric. She lost her main job and was only working part-time as an admin assistant. She called her best guy friend Bee and was crying on the phone about losing her job and losing her relationship.

She couldn't understand why this was happening to her. Why she was dealt this much pain and hurt by a man she thought truly loved her.

Maria just went on and on, on the phone in the bedroom for hours telling her best friend that she didn't deserve any of this, and why would God allow her to go through this much pain.

Maria was crying and crying she had no idea what she was going to do. She didn't want any of Marcus money because she knew she had to be strong. She had to stand her ground no matter how broken she was.

She continued to cry, and her best friend said it's going to be okay. Maria said how, what am I going to do. As she spoke those words God has never failed me, she began to see twenty-dollar bills fall from above her, she stopped crying because she didn't know where the money was falling from.

She told her best friend she would call him back. She looked up and Eric's cat Starlight was up in the closet in the bedroom and had scratched money that was hidden in the closet over to the edge and it was falling out on top of Maria.

Maria called Eric to her room and pushed him up in the closet and told him to push over anything else he saw in the closet. He pushed over $40,000.00 Maria was so happy. She said I know there is a God. Eric and Maria were so happy.

Maria called her best friend back and told him what had happen, she said there was $40,000.00 dollars in my bedroom closet, Eric's cat always jumped up in the closet and I would get mad at her, but today was truly a blessing and I'm happy she went up there.

Her best friend couldn't believe it he said you have always had an angel watching over you. God has always aligned you with a blessing. Maria agreed and said that she was moving she said she has had all she can take of that apartment.

A co-worker she worked with lived in an apartment on Olney Ave. over by B Street. so Maria and Eric moved in the following month, and was happy because no one knew where they were.

They even took Starlight too. Maria found a nice little church around the corner and started attending regularly with Eric she knew that she had to start living a better life and trusting God with her future. Marcus kept calling her phone, but Maria would not answer.

Marcus big show was about to go down in AC Maria had a little bit of change and said she might go. Let me go see what he is screaming about with comedy at this show. Maria asked Lacy if she wanted to go to the comedy show in AC Lacy said bet girl, we there.

Maria booked a night in AC at the Showboat Hotel and casino. She arrived there with bells on. The comedy show was further up the boardwalk, at boardwalk hall. Lacy and Maria would walk the short walk up there they were excited to be in the building.

CHAPTER TWENTY -FOUR

"The Jokes on you"

Marcus was getting ready for his big show, and he had Kaye with him, she was dressed in a red maxi dress with a slit on the side, he had on all black with a red blazer. He was excited at some of the material he had for his show. He guaranteed that there would be a lot of tears at his event.

Meanwhile Sharon, Monique, Rose, and Lisa all received an invite to the comedy show. They were each there unaware of each others existence.

When the show began it was a lot of laughter Marcus was hosting and announcing each comedian as they hit the stage. An hour went by and finally Marcus was about to hit the stage and do his thing all eyes were on him.

Sharon, Kaye, Monique, Rose, Lisa and Maria sitting in different areas of the arena but glued to the performance that was about to go down.

And now coming to the stage your very own comedian Marcus Hall everyone started clapping and going wild waiting to hear what he had to say.

Hey Atlantic City, Philly, and New York what's up? Make some noise, everybody started screaming and clapping louder, he started off with his first joke and then his second the audience was laughing so hard and giving him mad respect. But then came the story joke, he started off by saying its not fun messing around with a lot of ladies.

Running here and there fucking this one at work and going home to fuck the next while leaving her laid out on her back to go and fuck another one. That's a lot of fucking around (the audience laughed)

Some men put their fist in the air. He continued yeah! I have fucked around a lot felt well though my dick was a happy dick.

My dick was so happy that I was in strip clubs and bedrooms one after another, sleeping here and there up in this pussy and that ass, like it was no tomorrow. But truth is there was a tomorrow.

Tomorrow was filled with abortions and lies I was a man fucking around because I had no excuse or reason to be faithful. You see when I was thirteen years old, I was in a car accident it left me severely damaged in my penis area, my testicles were almost detached, the doctor had to stitch my shit back together.

I was told I would never have children, every test
they took came up negative for a sperm count.
They said listen it will never happen. I don't care
how many vaginas you go in or how many women
say that they are pregnant it would be a 2% chance
of you ever becoming a father.

So of course, I spent my entire life trying to
prove them wrong, and every year I went back to
take their test the doctor said the same damn thing,
sorry Mr. Hall you have no sperm in there. I started
laughing so hard I was beginning to think I was
crazy. (The audience laughs)

As they laughed harder Marcus continued his
jokes, he began to reenact every woman that he had
sitting in the audience and the encounter he had
with them Monique, Sharon, Rose, Kaye and Lisa
who was currently telling him she was pregnant.
Maria was in the audience but had never been
pregnant by Marcus.

He began to get teary eyed in the audience when
speaking about the baby boy that he now has. He
said quickly even though I know the bastard isn't
mine, he is the only child from birth that I will ever
know and have a chance to claim as my own.
Kaye's face was a ghost.

He continued on by saying that every woman he had ever been with was a liar. He said these women falsified and tricked him out of money, he said I could have said no, I could have said I know that's not my baby you are carrying but I didn't I just knew in my heart that I was being played and used just like I was Playing and using them.

I am not proud of the games I played or the lies I told yet I am hurt as a man to stand here and say that women aren't shit. Yawl lie to get money with the abortion game, and some of you really slept with those other dudes and got pregnant.

Yes, I knew it wasn't mine, and now you know it was never mine either. (The audience applauds louder at the jokes.) He received a standing ovation.

As Monique, Sharon, Rose, Kaye and Lisa looked on wondering if it was a joke he told or was it all the truth.

The Comedian (Look Who's Laughing Now)

Are You?

The End

The Comedian

(Look Who's Laughing Now)

Knowledge Is Learned

Angela M. Smith

Made in the USA
Middletown, DE
10 November 2021